P9-BBQ-273

# THE
# visible
# LIBRARIAN

*Asserting Your Value with Marketing and Advocacy*

# JUDITH A. SIESS

**AMERICAN LIBRARY ASSOCIATION**
Chicago
2003

Design and composition by ALA Editions in Bookman and Formata Regular using QuarkXPress 5.0 on a PC platform

Printed on 50-pound white offset, a pH-neutral stock, and bound in 10-point cover stock by Batson Printing

The paper used in this publication meets the minimum requirements of American National Standard for Information Sciences—Permanence of Paper for Printed Library Materials, ANSI Z39.48-1992.∞

**Library of Congress Cataloging-in-Publication Data**

Siess, Judith A.
    The visible librarian : asserting your value with marketing and advocacy /
  Judith A. Siess ; with a foreword by Kathy Dempsey.
       p.  cm.
  Includes bibliographical references and index.
  ISBN 0-8389-0848-9
    1. Libraries—Public relations. 2. Libraries—Marketing.
  3. Advertising—Libraries. 4. Libraries and readers.  I. Title.
  Z716.3.S54 2003
  021.7—dc21                           2003001922

Printed in the United States of America

07   06   05   04          5    4    3    2

# CONTENTS

# FOREWORD

by Kathy Dempsey

If you're reading this sentence, let me congratulate you. You're obviously among those of us who "get it." You realize that it's essential to publicize library services and to market them seriously. You may be an old hand at this, hoping this book will catch you up with the current school of thought. (It will.) Or you may be a novice at library marketing, thinking that you need one text that will explain the whole concept to you, convince you that it matters, and teach you how to play the game. (This will.) Either way, here you are. Welcome.

I think this is the right book at the right time. Why? As the author explains in the introduction, "Information at the desktop is no longer necessarily connected to a library or librarian in the user's mind. We are becoming more and more 'invisible.'" That's a great way to summarize one of today's biggest challenges.

Another reason that this book works now is that marketing seems to be getting more attention these days (and it's about time). It's been in the literature enough that it's become more demystified and more acceptable. We've come to realize that it's not just for big organizations with big money. By now we've seen enough examples to realize that any type of library can do interesting publicity and marketing—not only the local public library, but also corporate info centers, small special libraries, one-person libraries, school libraries, and academic libraries of all shapes and sizes. Also, more awards recognize these skills now. In fact, a new international marketing award was created and presented

KATHY DEMPSEY has been the editor of the *Marketing Library Services* newsletter since 1994. In addition, she edits *Computers in Libraries* magazine, speaks about library marketing, and writes for various industry publications including *Information World Review* in the United Kingdom. Previously, she worked in public and academic libraries.

for the first time in 2002 by the International Federation of Library Associations and Institutions (IFLA) and 3M. And when industry giants like IFLA and 3M do something, you'd better take notice.

On the not-so-bright side, unfortunate occurrences have also helped to draw attention to the need for librarians to become more visible. For a few years now, you've watched the number of your colleagues shrink as their employers cut back on staff and budgets, or they outsourced information services, or they (foolishly) closed the library or information center altogether. This frightening trend has been helped along in no small way by that insidious Internet rumor. (Yes, this book will give you some hints on what to do when someone says the *I* word to you.)

You can live in denial if you're watching budgets and resources dwindle slowly over time. But 2002 brought a bigger wake-up call that was hard for anyone to ignore. What I've come to call "the Washington State Library debacle" changed the whole playing field when a governor in a budget crisis figured he could eliminate the whole state library to save money. It was a bad play on his part, and thankfully—through the power of grassroots activism, strong campaigning, and powerful marketing—the library won the right to exist (barely). Problem was, these librarians and their excellent services had been invisible to most of the people who controlled the money. Those people in Washington learned that it was very dangerous to be invisible, and they learned it the hard way. That's another reason why this book is so essential now. We've been shown quite clearly that invisibility can be our downfall.

And now, if you're reading this, you have also come to believe that you need to be more visible. Not only do you "get it," but you've decided that you can't sit on the sidelines anymore. You intend to read this book and get into the game. I'm glad, because our team can use all the help it can get. Consider this your playbook. And consider author Judith A. Siess your able coach.

This text is valuable for several reasons. Foremost, I think it's great because it pulls together the knowledge of an enormous number of people who know this library marketing game. Over the last couple of decades, if somebody has said something about this topic—or thought it or written it or recommended it or done it—it's in here. If you don't have time to go back and read all the best articles and papers and books on the subject, don't worry. Now you don't have to. You've got a wonderfully organized summary of all the best practices in marketing library services right here.

Granted, this is a deep topic, and there's a lot of ground to cover. So nary a word is wasted here; they're all important. To deliver all the greatest wisdom on the subject, sometimes quote marks open and close with dizzying speed, but don't let that intimidate you. The concepts are not hard to grasp. This book doesn't contain difficult theories or futuristic pie-in-the-sky. It's all real-world stuff that you can understand and act upon. There's a lot to learn, but you don't have to know it all or do it all right away. Find the plays that fit your situation, the ideas that fit your needs and organization, and start implementing them now, a bit at a time. You *can* learn this, and you can trust Siess to lead you.

While you're studying to become more visible, you'll learn many things:

- When to market, and to whom
- How to defend against "It's all on the Internet"
- Ways to measure and prove your value, with real numbers
- How to argue against the common excuses for not marketing
- How to price your services
- How to segment different types of customers to serve them better
- Ideas for inexpensive promotional items to give away
- How to size up your competition
- How to write a solid publicity plan
- The five essential parts of a press release
- How your website can be a better publicity vehicle
- Why training can be great for your image
- How you can do your part to improve the plight of the profession and help make all librarians more visible

You need this book; every librarian does. Because you need to be visible and proactive and strong willed. You, as a librarian or information professional or knowledge manager working in the twenty-first century, need to stand up and speak out. You dare not be the Invisible Librarian. (Or you may find yourself with the invisible paycheck!) You need to learn how to be more seen and heard than many of you have been in the past, and this book can teach you how to do it.

Don't worry: marketing doesn't have to be like rabid activism or political campaigning. And it doesn't have to be a dirty word. But it is a word you have to face. You can do it, and you can be good at it. Join the team. Let this book show you how to become *The Visible Librarian.*

# INTRODUCTION

"What can you do to keep from being invisible to your managers, colleagues, potential users, and the business world in general?" (Dempsey 2002, 77)

"Libraries do not market; occasionally they advertise what they already provide. However, increasingly we now anti-advertise, when budget cuts have made it difficult to maintain levels of service. [We allow] the budget to define the program rather than have the program define the budget." (White 1997, 116)

## WHY THIS BOOK WAS WRITTEN

In the late twentieth and early twenty-first century, libraries are no longer a given. Some librarians have known this for a long time. For example, hospital accreditation rules used to require a library on-site and a degreed librarian on staff. However, recent changes in the accreditation guidelines only require "access" to medical information. When Baker and McKenzie, the largest law firm in the United States, closed its library, law firms all over the country followed suit. And the not-for-profit sector is not immune. Branches of public libraries are being closed, school libraries merged or combined with the public library or even eliminated. Even in the "safe" academic library, positions are being eliminated and branches or departmental libraries closed.

Why is this happening? Because librarians have not marketed themselves and their services to management—to the decision makers. We have also not been good at advocacy. We don't speak up for ourselves and recruit others to do the same; we don't acquire and use library champions. Why don't we market and practice advocacy? There are several reasons.

1. We don't realize how important it is to our continued well-being and even survival, even though we've been told to market over and over.
2. We don't know how. Few library schools teach marketing (and when they do, it often is only how to write brochures and fliers and signs and such), and advocacy is almost unheard of. There have been numerous books written with library or information "marketing," "publicity," "public relations," or "advocacy" in their titles. But are they read? Or put into action?
3. We don't have time. Time is a precious commodity for most librarians. Because marketing and advocacy do not stand at the reference or circulation desk and command our attention, or send memos or e-mails requesting action, or call on the telephone or threaten to strike, as do the other demands on the librarian's time, they are sent to the bottom of the priority list. Of course the librarian's time is eventually freed up—when the library is closed.

Libraries have been threatened before and they have survived. Why should we be more concerned now?

1. The rise of the Internet. Is there a librarian living who hasn't heard "It's all on the Internet and it's all free" at least a dozen times? Of course *we* know that it isn't *all* on the Internet and, assuming the user's time and convenience is worth something, it certainly isn't free, but how do we convince our users and our funders?
2. The apparent popularity of end-user searching. Users can now search not only the Internet, but also many subscription databases themselves. Often they do not realize who has given them this access—the library. In a corporation, the librarian (if there is one) is nearly always the one who chooses, negotiates for, and places the databases on the intranet or portal. Public libraries give cardholders access to a myriad of databases at no cost to the user. Before, the user would have either had to pay for access or do without the information. A hospital or medical school would not survive long without access to Medline or other medical databases. I cannot imagine a law firm and law school without Westlaw or LexisNexis, and most subscribe to both. Who chooses, purchases, maintains, and trains users in the use of these tools? Librarians.
3. Many libraries are going "virtual," that is, eliminating their physical presence in organizations. Whether virtualization is the idea of the librarian or is forced on him or her by management, the

result is the same. Information at the desktop is no longer necessarily connected to a library or librarian in the user's mind. We are becoming more and more "invisible."

4. Corporations (and other institutions) are getting very good at and comfortable with outsourcing. Human resources and information technology are two of the more commonly outsourced departments. To many executives, outsourcing of the library is the next logical step.

5. A poor economic situation and increasing emphasis on the bottom line make constant downsizing a well-accepted (if short-sighted) management practice. "Libraries usually aren't tied to the revenue-generating side of the business" (Corcoran 2002, 76). Downsizing even happens in not-for-profit organizations like public libraries, schools, and hospitals.

6. Technology has made it easier to find and obtain information. The computer is a direct contributor (or enabler) of factors 1 through 3. In some ways it has made our job so easy that people think "anyone" can do it. And we haven't done a very good job of proving otherwise.

## WHY DID I WRITE THIS BOOK?

My work experience has been primarily in solo or one-person libraries. Over the last twenty years I have seen more and more libraries become one-person libraries—because of downsizing. At the same time, many one-person libraries (and larger ones as well) are disappearing altogether. Although we live in the information age and management is aware of the importance of information, they still don't understand how important it is to have an information professional in charge of it. Even when they think they have put an information person in charge of the organization's information needs, we often find that this person is a computer professional—not a librarian.

How can I, a special librarian, presume to speak to public or academic or school or hospital or law librarians? The way I see it, what makes a library special is its ability to know and customize its services to a specific user population, whether that population is a community, university, company, hospital, or law firm. Therefore, *all* libraries are special libraries. Marketing is marketing, whether in a special library or a public library, and advocacy is advocacy, whether in the halls of Congress or in your boss's office. The principles are the same; it is the application and language that are different.

# DEFINITIONS

> "If a boy tells his girl he loves her, that's advertising. If he tells
> her how great he is, that's promotion. If her friends tell her how
> great he is, that's public relations!" (Fox, former president of
> the Public Relations Society of America, in Usherwood 1981, 6)

Often *marketing* is confused with *publicity* or *public relations. Advocacy*
is confused with *lobbying.* The definitions that follow are some of the
ways that others have defined these terms.

## Marketing

"Marketing is asking who are you, what do you want, how can I best
deliver it to you, tell you about it and at what price? Marketing is what
you should do *before* you do public relations. If you don't know who your
clientele is (or should be) and what they want, how can you tell them
what you can do for them? Also, do you really know what your services
are (or should be)? Do you want to promote your searching or your document delivery or the breadth and depth of your collection? What does
your potential audience already know about your library? What do they
think about it and its services?" (Cavill 2001, 90).

"Marketing is too frequently defined in language that actually means
'promotion.' [Marketing is] a series of activities that begins with a community analysis to determine the needs of the consumers and ends with
the library's communication to the community relating the products
created to respond to those needs" (Weingand 1994, 314).

"Marketing is designed to get people to want something they don't
have" (White 1984, 177).

"Marketing is much more than selling. It is an exchange of value in
which both parties gain something" (Brown 1997, 75).

## Promotion or Publicity

"Promotion consists of any activity that alerts the community to the new
collection and service and suggests how these resources will benefit the
people who use them" [of course this applies to existing services as well]
(Baker and Manbeck 2002, 109).

"[Promotion is] communicating to present and potential clients that
the library has identified community needs and developed cost-effective
products and methods of distribution that respond to those needs"
(Weingand 1994, 145–46).

"Promotion includes: Public relations: overall library-client interaction; Publicity: free news coverage; Advertising: paid publicity; Incentives: free trials, coupons; and Atmospherics: ambience or environment [whether at physical or electronic sites]" (Weingand 1995, 314–15).

## Public Relations

"Public Relations is saying this is who we are, this is what we do, for whom and when. With this tool we sell our services to our target audience. Be careful to phrase PR in a way that relates directly to that audience. This will differ depending on whether you are talking to executives, the public, or children. Your professional organization will have plenty of materials that you can use for your PR campaign" (Cavill 2001, 90).

Public relations seeks both to inform and to influence. Objectives of library public relations are to obtain or increase funding, increase awareness, improve public image, get the message to staff, and create confidence (Usherwood 1981).

"PR is the art of persuading your audience to: 1) be aware of you; and 2) form positive associations with your name" (Seacord 1999, 6).

The slogan of my library was "The Bailey Library . . . it's more than you thought." At a company meeting I rose to ask a question, and the chief operating officer replied, "Yes, Judy, it's more than you thought." Everyone laughed. I was very embarrassed, but my boss leaned over and told me not to worry. The laughter meant that everyone had heard the slogan and knew about the library. The power of public relations.

"[Public relations is] influencing perception, attitude, and opinion by transmitting information about the benefits of using the library's product and services" (Weingand 1994, 145).

## Advocacy

"Advocacy is about saying to decision-makers, potential partners, funders [or] any stakeholder, 'Your agenda will be greatly assisted by what we have to offer.' Advocacy is about getting support from those who are in a position to help you and your library. If you don't sell them, then you won't have anything to sell to your target audience" (Cavill 2001, 91).

"Advocacy is the act of pleading for or supporting a change in an existing system which will produce results that are permanent and will benefit future users of the system. An advocate is one who speaks or acts on behalf of another or in support of a cause" (Bingham in Kirchner 1999, 844).

## *MY* DEFINITIONS

*The Visible Librarian* uses the following definitions. *Marketing* is determining who you serve and with what products (chapter 2). *Publicity* is getting the word out that you can help people do their jobs better-cheaper-faster (chapter 3). *Public relations* is talking to people about their needs and your strengths (chapter 4). In "Advocacy: Putting It All Together" (chapter 5), all of the above are combined to make sure we get the resources that we need to provide excellent information products and services to our customers. In addition, advocacy includes all the aspects of professionalism that we can use to accomplish the above: dress, attitude, continuing education, networking, and working to improve the image of our profession.

One final word. You can't learn to market by studying or reading—even by reading this book. This book will only give you some of the basics. You learn by doing—finding out what works for you, your library, and your clients.

# 1 The Primacy of Customer Service and Other Basics

"Give the people what they want. It's their library." (Scilken in Deitch 1984, 207)

"High standards of customer service create higher visibility for the information service unit. It is this enhanced visibility that will lead to better positioning in the organization." (Gupta and Jambhekar 2002, 27)

## SELLING THE INVISIBLE: WHAT SETS LIBRARIANS APART . . . CUSTOMER SERVICE

The concept of selling the invisible comes from a book with the same title by Harry Beckwith. The invisible is service. The subtitle of Beckwith's book is *A Field Guide to Modern Marketing.* Modern marketing is all about the customer. "Unless customers and the collection come together in a way both interesting and meaningful to customers, the library is nothing more than an expensive warehouse" (Hernon and Altman 1998, 6). Most librarians, especially those in public libraries, are unaccustomed to calling the people they serve *customers.* For years we have used the term *patron* or sometimes *user.* Perhaps we have avoided the term *customer* because it implies "an exchange [of money] occurring between the library and the people using the service" (Hernon and Altman 1998, 3). Yet the relationship with the customer has become so important that the Malcolm Baldridge National Quality Award "values customer and market knowledge, customer satisfaction, and customer-focused results, as a combination, higher than any other single measure for the award" (Hernon and Whitman 2001, ix).

The time has come to change both our terminology and our thinking. As Christine M. Koontz (2002, 4) notes, library users are now also customers who demand, choose, and select among information products. Customers have expectations, including the expectation of being appreciated. They expect to get what they ordered and are not interested in why the library cannot deliver. They expect the information we deliver to be accurate, timely, and of value. They expect friendly employees, an attractive and easy-to-use facility, a wide and well-reasoned selection of resources, and a host of other wide-ranging and ever-changing services and products.

Darlene E. Weingand (1998, 15) defines four levels of customer service. "Basic: A building containing print and audiovisual materials. Expected: Competent assistance of staff in finding information and materials; clean, attractive surroundings. Desired: Needed materials secured through interlibrary loan from another library; cheerful, helpful, and pleasant staff attitudes. Unanticipated: Referral to another person or agency; information available through computer linkups." Dinesh K. Gupta and Ashok Jambhekar (2002, 30) add levels at the top and bottom, and the lowest level is miserable service: "The employee actually goes out of his way to irritate the customer." Even higher than Weingand's unanticipated level is exceptional service, when the interaction is enjoyable, the staff courteous, and the customer leaves wanting to return.

Leonard Berry (in Reuben and Carter 2001) described five necessary elements of customer service. (All five must be present for success.) "Solve your customers' problems. Treat customers with respect. Connect with your customers' emotions. Set fairest, not the lowest prices. Save your customers' time." Customers also want to feel in control. They want the process to be easy and for us to pay attention, read between the lines, listen actively, and be patient and tactful. And finally, your customers want answers, not information. They want their problems solved.

Corporations like Disney, amazon.com, and McDonald's have raised the service bar for everyone, including libraries. "More people every day have experienced extraordinary service. They have seen world-class service, and now every service has to accept it. A service that does not jump to meet these rising expectations will have a small revolution and a customer exodus on its hands" (Beckwith 1997, 9). What may have been perceived as excellent service a few years ago is not acceptable today. Beckwith goes on to say that you should let your clients, not your industry or your ego, set your service standards: "Customer service is in the eye of the beholder." If they don't think it's good, it isn't (Talley and Axelroth 2001, 10). We aren't the best ones to judge our own service, either. It is not a bad idea to take Beckwith's suggestion and "assume your service is bad. It can't hurt, and it will force you to improve" (1997, 6). In the past, customer service wasn't a major issue in libraries because it didn't have to be. They came to us when they needed us—or so we thought. Today our customers have choices in the acquisition of information, and the library or information center may not be the first choice.

Do our users know good service when they see it? They may not. Expectations of libraries are usually quite low, and "users do not know what good library service is and, therefore, are not in a position to know when they do not receive it" (White 1984, 146). In fact, some believe that those who do have higher expectations may lower these expectations as they encounter lower levels of service and give up on getting anything better. I disagree. People know good service when they receive it; it's just that they don't see it very often and are so amazed by it that they don't demand it of every encounter.

One sector from which we almost never expect excellent customer service is the airline industry. We have come to expect—and accept—poor service as an unfortunate aspect of air travel. But there are exceptions. My husband and I were traveling from Cleveland to Dallas. Because of the increased surveillance after September 11, 2001, it took about forty-five minutes to clear the security check at the entrance to the concourse. When we boarded the plane, the flight attendant announced that we would be taking off at least ninety minutes after the scheduled departure time. However, he added, those who had connections that would not be made were *already* rebooked on new flights, and the new gates and departure times would be given to the passengers as they left the plane in Dallas. I was in disbelief! I had never heard of an airline taking such initiative and preemptively taking care of a potential problem for the passenger. Now, why is this not standard procedure? Why should passengers have to take care of this problem themselves once they reach their destination? And why aren't passengers demanding that the airlines provide this service? The answer of course is that if none of the airlines provide this service, the passengers will accept it, and meekly at that. We have been "trained" by the airlines to accept poor service. Passengers do not really have a viable alternative. If even one airline dared to break out of the pack and offer exceptional service, the others would have to follow, and the bar would be raised.

"Anyone who has worked a reference desk has seen users pleased with a quick and mediocre answer when, with a bit more time and effort, they could get a better one." Roy Tennant calls this "satisficing," being only good enough (2001, 39). There are many competitors for the information dollar: the Internet, direct sales by vendors to the end-user, asking a nearby colleague, making a phone call to another library or information center, and so forth. But the library's biggest and most dangerous competitor is simply *doing without.* White put it this way: "Librarians must bear in mind that a report due on Monday morning will be delivered Monday morning with or without library input; the user will simply proceed as if all available information has indeed been located" (1984, 147–48). We are not necessary to the completion of the report. The customer has the ultimate power—to ignore us completely.

## Creating Lasting Customer Relationships

Larry X. Besant and Deborah Sharp (2000) describe three kinds of relationships between a customer and the library. The service encounter involves person-to-person contact, for example, at the circulation or information desk. The electronic relationship is person-to-machine, usually through the website. The final type is the knowledge relationship, as is typified by the reference question. Beckwith (2000, 170–223) lists eight keys to lasting relationships.

1. Natural affinity. Clients look for someone who is the most like them, people they *like.*
2. Trust, predictability, consistency, and honesty.
3. Speed. Get fast, then faster. You cannot deliver your product to the customer too fast.
4. Apparent expertise. Look the part, dress the part. Show them your expertise, no matter how specialized. Don't belittle yourself. Act confidently.
5. Sacrifice. Give in. The customer is always right.
6. Completeness. "Know how or know who." Be a one-stop shop.
7. The magic words. "Thank you"—say it often. Say "You're welcome" and mean it. Use the client's name—often. Take a cue from McDonald's and ask the library equivalent of "Would you like fries with that?"—"Did you find what you were looking for?"
8. Passion. It's contagious. Clients will catch your passion and become passionate about your library, too.

The best relationship between a customer and a library is the partnership. A partnership relationship takes more work than a customer relationship. In a true partnership, each partner has an interest in the other's success and does what he or she can to ensure that success. The hallmark of the partnership is loyalty. "Libraries need to create more loyal customers, yet many public librarians seem to talk more about attracting nonusers than keeping present customers happy or finding out why previous customers no longer return" (Hernon and Altman 1998, 13). This is very shortsighted. It is a maxim of marketing that it is much more expensive to acquire a new customer than it is to retain one. Even if your customers are satisfied with your services and products, someone else may be just a bit more responsive, convenient, less expensive, or just different. The customer may not be unhappy, but he may not be excessively happy either and will be easy prey for a savvy competitor. A partner will forgive a mistake easier than a customer and won't jump ship at the first bad experience. Why do companies lose customers? The American Society for Quality Control found that 1 percent die, 5 percent move away, 7 percent are lured elsewhere, 9 percent go to the competition, and 15 percent leave because of a quality problem, but an astonishing 63 percent leave because they feel ignored! (Newell 1997, 137).

Getting to know your customers, their needs and preferences, gives you an edge on your competitors. The relationship you've built makes it more likely they'll stay with you—and even buy from or use you more because they don't want to have to train another supplier. Listen to customers; really listen. Listen as if you care. Keep a card file of customer likes, interests, and personal information. For example: Dr. Smith: surgeon, likes lots of articles, doesn't mind waiting for right information; Mrs. Jones: gardener (especially roses), friend of board chairman, comment on her weight loss; Professor Brown: usually sends a grad student for information but doesn't mind if you call him for clarification, loves detective stories about libraries. Say "Tell me more," or ask such questions as "What do you suggest?" "Is this helpful?" "How can I fix this?" "What will it take to make you happy?" Then do it if you can. If filling a request or solving a problem will take a while, keep the customer informed of your progress. The personal touch is perhaps our most important selling point, especially in contrast with the impersonality and anonymity of the Internet.

Library history, education, and theory tell us that all customers should be treated alike, but this is just not practical in real life. As in George Orwell's *Animal Farm,* some customers are more equal than others. "No information center can effectively serve every single employee in the company. Some segments may generate greater financial impact than others, some may be more strategically important, and others may have higher potential" (Brown 1997, 76). Telling the chief executive officer (CEO) (or managing partner or chief of the medical staff or president or mayor or superintendent of schools) that he or she will have to wait while you answer a question from a secretary (or summer intern or resident or clerk or member of the public or teacher) may be egalitarian, but it may also be a shortcut to the unemployment line. One corporate library even segmented its market into "priority" users and the rest of the company. Priority users got full service, including access to the librarian's services. The rest were welcome in the library but only on a self-service basis (St. Clair 1993). All services must be appropriate but not necessarily equal.

## Barriers to Customer Service

One barrier libraries put between the library and the customer is the classification system. "It should be noted that no other service-oriented organization requires its users to learn an arbitrary system in order to access needed materials. The . . . library should be more concerned with arranging its collection for ease of use than with strict compliance to the Library of Congress [or Dewey decimal] classification system" (Shimpock-Vieweg 1992, 77). Exact call numbers are less necessary with online catalogs. Does a call number make it easier to retrieve materials? Only if items are shelved correctly and the user understands the system. We should use our valuable classification skills and limited time to assign more customer-specific subject headings.

Librarians also hold attitudes that are barriers to customer service excellence. Libraries are inherently good. There is no competition. Libraries will continue to exist and be funded without regard to service level or efficiency. Customers will use the library because it's free—or perceived to be so—regardless of quality of service. Library work is not measurable, or not in terms of quality or outcome for the user. Apathy can be caused by a service orientation that was either never there or fell victim to librarian burnout. The brush-off, a lack of personal involvement in users' needs, can result in a curt and incomplete answer to a reference question. Condescension, found most often in academic libraries (but by no means limited to them), is usually manifested by giving the user what we think he or she *should* have, not necessarily what he or she wants or needs. Finally, there is "thinly disguised contempt [TDC]," called by Tom Peters "the biggest barrier to sustainable superior performance" (in Barter 1994, 6). This can be expressed as "if the patron can't find something, it's *his or her* fault." Another form of TDC is the notion that the users must recognize the value of library service. In fact, it is we who need to demonstrate our value. Here is an excellent example of the proper customer service attitude—just substitute *customer* for *patient*.

What Is a Patient?

A patient is the most important person in the institution—in person or by mail.

A patient is not dependent on us—we are dependent on them.

A patient is not an interruption of our work—it is the purpose of it.

The patient is not an outsider to our business—they are our business.

The patient is not someone to argue or match wits with.

The patient is a person and not a statistic. It is our job to satisfy them.

(William E. Lower, M.D., the Cleveland Clinic Foundation, February 1921, found on a sign at the admitting desk)

A barrier that Tennant (2001, 39) calls the "convenience catastrophe" is the result of the deliberate efforts of librarians: "Because of stagnant or declining budget allocations, many libraries have made conscious attempts to foster customers' self-sufficiency." This is sometimes called "empowerment," or even "library education" (Hernon and Altman 1998, 19). Do our customers really want to do our jobs or do they want service? Answers, not search tips? Solutions, not access? Leave self-service for the grocery store. Our customers want and need intermediaries; they want and need service.

## Customer Service Expectations: Learning from Dissatisfied Customers

"It is important to note that no matter how hard you try for the 0% failure rate there will always be someone who will walk away from you dissatisfied. As a result, it is necessary that you devise a recovery plan" (Wagner 1997, 32). Be open to criticism. Make changes. What's more, complaints are good. "One of the surest signs of a bad or declining relationship with a customer is the absence of complaints. Nobody is ever *that* satisfied, especially not over an extended period of time. The customer is either not being *candid* or not being *contacted*" (Levitt, Harvard University professor, in Bell 1994, 111). In fact, people who have encountered a service problem and had it corrected can be more loyal than those who've never had a problem. When there is a problem, you must provide a way for the consumer to get assistance, such as a toll-free number that is answered by a human or a website with interactive scripts that produce answers. Don't just sit and wait for customers to comment on service; they probably won't. If service is bad, they will just go away. If it's good, they think that's just how it should be. Few unhappy customers will complain to you; the rest will complain to others. A satisfied customer may tell one or two people; a dissatisfied one will tell about ten. Why don't people complain? (1) They may not know how. Make it easy, use comment cards, Web forms, toll-free phone numbers. (2) They think it's a waste of time; it won't do any good. Act on complaints: give feedback to all complainers if they give a contact point; when you change something, announce it as "in response to your complaints, we have done X." Libraries don't die a violent, sudden death; they fade away as customers stop coming. Often by the time the manager realizes that there is a problem, it is too late. Don't let that happen to you. Actively solicit customer feedback—and make changes accordingly. American retail legend Marshall Field wrote, "Those who enter to buy, support me. Those who come to flatter, please me. Those who complain, teach me how I may please others so more will come. Only those hurt me who are displeased but do not complain. They refuse me permission to correct my errors and improve service" (in Wilson 1991, 119).

Beckwith cautions, "If your goal is satisfied clients, your goal is far too modest" (2000, 68). Satisfied is the *least* customers expect. You want "surprised and delighted" customers. How do your customers express satisfaction? In many ways, but there is only one that counts—with their dollars (or yen or pounds or euros or pesos or whatever currency your organization runs on). Compliments and return customers are important, as are increasing circulation and searches or document delivery requests, but if the library is not funded, it can't continue to exist. That doesn't mean you can ignore everyone but the funders of your library; satisfying your regular customers and increasing their numbers are still vital. Satisfied customers talk to their bosses (with a little prodding from you), who talk to *their* bosses, and on up the chain of command to the big boss who makes the decisions about library funding.

What about the *un*satisfied customer? There are some people who will never be satisfied, no matter how hard you try. Accept this fact and get on with life. You cannot please everyone. Just as in Olympic scoring, ignore the few who hate everything you do and the few who love everything you do and concentrate on those in the middle. Although you should try to personalize your services and products for your customers, you don't have time to do this perfectly for every customer. You need to let them know this. Explain that you have many customers and limited time and that you will do the best you can for them, but they need to be somewhat flexible.

Beware of the danger of ever-rising expectations. Just as we librarians quickly take new services or products from our vendors as forming the new baseline and then demand even more from our suppliers, so do our customers. Customer expectations also change as they are exposed to other providers. For example, FedEx and UPS have raised the bar for the U.S. Postal Service, just as the Web has raised it for the library

(Hernon and Whitman 2001). The Web has accustomed our customers to instant information at the desktop. It has created the expectation that all information can—and will—be delivered instantly. Can you meet this expectation? Should you? One solution is to move "from the satisfied to the self-satisfied consumer" (McKenna 1997, 148). Instead of waiting for *you* to solve the problem, give your customers the tools they need to solve it themselves. Of course you still will have to choose the appropriate tools and resources and train the users on the efficient use of them.

Another kind of dissatisfied customer is one who is simply a difficult person. Sometimes this person is one who is "always" difficult; sometimes he or she is just being difficult in this particular frustrating situation. Sometimes a problem with a difficult customer is just a matter of mismatched styles of communication, personality, or expectations. To defuse an angry customer, first acknowledge the person is upset. You don't have to agree with him or her; just acknowledge his or her fury. Then make a sad-glad statement such as, "I'm sorry you're unhappy. Thank you for telling me." Show them you care. Next, make a positive statement, for example, "I will do something to solve this problem." Surprise them with action. Your next step is to ask the "magic question"—"What will make you happy?" Usually they will ask for something reasonable and doable. This will enable you to take the next step, making a settlement acceptable to both parties. To turn a dissatisfied customer into a really satisfied customer, take a bonus step—do something extra and unexpected (Wilson 1991).

## IMPLEMENTING A CUSTOMER SERVICE PLAN

Satisfying your customers is simple. Exceed their expectations. Keep doing what works and improve the rest. Then set about improving what was working. No matter how good your service is now, you should always ask how it could be better. Identify problems, using complaints and observation. Then get a commitment from your staff and management to improve service (or product) quality. Without this commitment, you will get nowhere. Implement a quality training program for your staff, either formally (probably necessary with a large staff) or informally. At the same time, establish clear channels of communication between you and your staff and between you and management. Make sure that everyone is on the same wavelength, has the same input, and is kept informed of all quality initiatives and changes in procedure or policy. If your staff is large, appoint a quality leader for each functional area. However, try to put as few layers between the lowest staff member and yourself.

Now it is time to set your objectives. Be specific. "Improving customer relations" is not an objective; "Reduce customer complaints about the document delivery service by 10 percent" is. It is better to start with a few easily achievable objectives that allow you to show early success. Then you can build on your successes with a more confident team. Next, evaluate the processes involved in the objectives. Where can they be improved? What will be the impact of these modifications on other processes? Write the new procedures or policies and train all staff involved in the new procedures. If there's a choice between making it easy for the staff or making it easy for the customer, always choose the customer. Make it very clear to the staff that customer service is a core task for every person. No one says, "That's not my responsibility" or "Sorry—I can't help you." Even the manager must be willing to answer phones, photocopy, and so forth—whatever it takes. Never ask your staff to do anything you would not be willing to do yourself. The CEO of Scandinavian Airlines, Jan Carlzon, said, "If you aren't serving the customer, your job is to be serving someone who is" (in Bell 1994, 181). Evaluate the new procedures. Are they working? Are they making a difference? Are there more modifications that can be made? Has the objective been met? Finally, repeat the entire process. Quality improvement is not a one-time activity; it is a continual process of evaluation, change, and reevaluation.

### Efficiency or Effectiveness: Doing Things Right versus Doing the Right Things

Quality improvement is a good thing. So is streamlining, efficiency, and improvements in productivity. But even a good thing can be overdone. There is a danger of productivity "tunnel vision," focusing on it to the exclusion of other measures (Phillips 1990, 151). Many of the problems in modern business are caused by the confusion between efficiency and effectiveness. *Efficiency* is working so as to minimize wasted labor, money, or time. *Effectiveness*, on the other hand, means examining a range of tasks, selecting the most important to be completed, and then completing it. In short, efficiency means doing things right, while effectiveness mean doing the right things. Efficiency—doing things right—is good, but effectiveness—doing the right things—is better. Doing the wrong things right is the epitome of wasted time.

Speaking of time, research has shown that 80 percent of our work (and the time it takes to do it) comes from only 20 percent of the tasks.

The trick is to make sure we are doing the *right* 20 percent. And when you do the right 20 percent the right way, well, that is productivity nirvana. (This 80/20 rule is called the Pareto principle. A good explanation of the Pareto principle is found in Richard Koch's *The 80/20 Principle: The Secret of Achieving More with Less.*) Use marketing research to find out what the right things are; then put them into order based on their importance—or priority. Now you can begin to streamline processes and improve quality service and staff productivity.

## CHANGE MANAGEMENT

> "Change hurts; indecision kills." (Miller in Mieszkowski 1999, 156)

> "Even if you're on the right track, you'll get run over if you just sit there." (Mark Twain)

Many of the concepts in this book require making changes in what you are doing or responding to changes in the marketplace or profession. Nowadays, not only is change constant, but the speed of change is constantly increasing. This situation is not likely to change. Vendors' products (and ours) are going to be changing rapidly—perhaps faster than we can be trained and train others. Not only do we have to deal with change, but we have to help those around us (our staff and colleagues and even our bosses) deal with it as well. The library must be able to change. It is far better to anticipate change than to lag behind, but don't change just for the sake of change. Change because the situation demands it. Make sure the change is worth the price (in money, time, or aggravation). Make sure the change will work within the organization or community as a whole—your library does not exist in a vacuum. Realize that change will, in all likelihood, cause a temporary drop in productivity. Plan for this consequence, and let your staff know that it is all right for this to occur—as long as it is only temporary.

Change management requires a gentle touch. It is often hard to get people to change who have been doing the same thing for a long time. They identify with what they do—it is their self-image. They have a lot invested in time and training. It's not the fear of the unknown that causes us to fear change, but the possibility of loss of comfort, of routine, of productivity, of relationships, of status or authority, of expertise, or of a job (Gallacher 1999, 6). Reassure them that yes, this will all be worth the trouble and that they will be rewarded for their efforts.

Allow them to participate in the change decision process. "In general, people with more power to understand and shape a change go through the cycle of responses more quickly" (12). There are seven stages of change (12):

1. Numbness, shock, immobilization, or feeling overwhelmed.
2. Denial. People may ignore the request for change or try to avoid it by saying, for instance, "We tried it before and it didn't work."
3. Depression, fear, defensiveness, or even outright hostility.
4. Acceptance. After people have worked through the first three states, they are able to discard the past and focus on the future.
5. Testing. At this point people will adapt to the situation, possibly even taking the initiative in suggesting responses to the changes.
6. Search for meaning. This is the process of establishing new procedures. Involve the participants.
7. Internalization. The changes are made a part of the normal routine, and the process of change is now complete.

## What Kinds of Changes in Our Libraries Might We Expect in the Future?

### FINANCIAL TRENDS

Because of the rising cost of health-care and deficit spending, funding is moving from states and the federal government to local governments. This will lead to even more inequities among public libraries and others dependent on federal or state funding.

As the cost of information drops and more people become able to access information themselves, they may not need the library as much. This will result in lower customer counts, reduced funding, and downsizing or elimination (or both) of some libraries.

### TECHNOLOGY TRENDS

More and more information is appearing in electronic form, leading to less dependence on and interest in print materials, our past strength. This will require us to operate and to think differently about information, customer service, and the role of the library.

When introducing new technology, make sure you provide it at the user's comfort level, not that of the software or the librarian. This is yet another instance of "the customer is always right."

We are moving "from computing to communication" (McKenna 1997, 22). This involves moving from a focus on tools (hardware, software) to a focus on solutions (results). Because many computer people are not known for their customer-service orientation, this represents a good opportunity for librarians to become more involved in technology applications.

According to Nicholas Negroponte of MIT, "Being digital will change the nature of mass media from a process of pushing bits at people to one of allowing people (or their computers) to pull at them" (in McKenna 1997, 63). What we should be creating is a system that makes the pull automatic, with no effort needed by the customer. The content provider (us) will determine the user's needs and automatically fill them. This really goes back to push but with the ability to change the information pushed on the fly.

## INFORMATION TRENDS

Knowledge management (KM) is just the most recent description of the value of integrating all the information in an organization within a logical and user-friendly system. Of course we librarians have known this and have been doing it for years. But management has finally figured it out. The only real innovation in KM has been the addition of intellectual capital (what's in people's heads) as part of the information matrix.

G. Edward Evans, Patricia Layzell Ward, and Bendik Ruggas (2000, 527) identify several challenges for the library of the future, including the end of "all and forever"—their term for *collecting*. We already have seen the rise of just-in-time document delivery. With the ease of supplying documents from the Web, the need for "just-in-case" collections is diminishing. We also will have to resolve some long-standing library issues: fee versus free, print versus electronic, and copyright.

## MANAGEMENT TRENDS

The rise of the individual requires the personalization or customization of information services and products. Based on our training in the art of the reference interview, librarians are poised to become major players.

The difficulties involved in designing, planning, and budgeting for unknown technologies and the increasing numbers of requests for virtual libraries leads us to ask, "How do we build libraries that nobody has seen before?" (Evans, Ward, and Ruggas 2000, 527). Or build virtual collections no one has imagined?

Globalization is a trend influencing special libraries and maybe others, too. It also affects organization or association libraries with global memberships, academic libraries providing distance learning, and school libraries that serve electronic pen pals or use global websites.

Management theory emphasizes the importance of long-range planning. However, sometimes it is better to think short term, especially in times of very rapid change or when the future is very uncertain—like now.

## CONSUMER TRENDS

We are seeing limits on growth; bigger is not necessarily better. The channels of information distribution are changing. Consumers' perception of value is changing, putting more emphasis on convenience and personalization. Time has become more valuable than money. Finally, we are seeing a change from generation X to gen Y. Who are these new consumers?

# 2 Doing the Groundwork: Marketing

"The overriding goal of marketing is to assure that the library will remain as an information center within the community." (Leerburger 1989, 8)

"Every act is a marketing act." (Beckwith 1997, 38)

## WHY MARKET?

If no one knows about your library and how it can help its community meet its goals, the library will not—and should not—continue to exist. It's that simple. The complicated part comes in communicating to potential customers the value of using the library. Chip R. Bell (1994) wrote, "Overlooked eventually can mean unemployed. Marketing means creating an awareness of your value." Referring to law libraries, Kathy Shimpock-Vieweg (1992, 67–68) reminded us that "marketing makes a library visible within the firm, ensures its continued survival and growth, and positions the library as an indispensable resource which fills a need that cannot be met elsewhere. In addition, marketing provides librarians with a vehicle to express their needs and accomplishments in a way that can be easily understood by others." As we know, the library is not always visible: "When someone discovers [my library] for the first time, I often hear him say it was the company's 'best-kept secret.' This is not how it should be!" (Swart 2000). "In a perfect world . . . the library would serve as both a real place worth spending time at and a virtual information center available 24 hours a day. . . . The library would be the top-of-the-list destination for information and pleasure seekers alike. . . . The truth is the library isn't on the radar screen of many people who think of themselves as information literate" (Sass 2002, 37).

Marketing is not something you can do in your spare time, with spare change. It is, or should be, an integrated system that covers everything from finding out what your customers need to evaluating how they perceive your products and services. It includes everything that the library does, from the day you open the doors. Your marketing efforts must be consistent in the message you are sending and in the way that you send it. You must take advantage of all the various forms of communication available to you. "The new marketing is more than a way of doing; it is a way of thinking. It begins with an understanding of the distinctive characteristics of services—their invisibility and intangibility—and of the unique nature of service prospects and users—their fear, their limited time, their sometimes illogical ways of making decisions, and their most important drives and needs" (Beckwith 1997, xx). Modern marketing's most basic principle is the supremacy of the customer. Only the user knows what information he or she needs. To provide anything less is not sufficient and will not keep you in business.

## WHO SHOULD MARKET?

Once you have accepted that marketing is vital to the success and continued existence of your library, the next step is determining *who* will do the marketing. There is only one answer: it must be done by you, the librarian. Not only are you the person best suited to do it, no one else will do it for you. You know your library better than anyone else. You know—or should know—your organization or community and customers better than an outsider possibly could. No one has more to gain from marketing or more to lose if you don't market. You can read books, take courses or workshops, or hire a marketing consultant. But *you* have to be in charge of the overall plan.

More and more we should see that part of the job of a librarian "is to enlighten users about the value of information and the potential—and limits—of information technology" (Dearstyne 2000, 34). This becomes even more important as newer generations of customers, raised on computers and used to searching the Internet for themselves, enter the workforce. We need to go on the offensive and attack the librarian stereotype and the myth that it is all free on the Internet. After all, the library of the twenty-first century is and must be run like a business. Fortunately, librarians now are better equipped to do this than ever before. Our training in the reference interview has taught us "all the basic elements of good sales technique—questioning and listening to find out the exact need, explaining what can be done in reply, and agreeing [to] a course of action" (Coote and Batchelor 1997, 24). But we must stop doing what we've always done. "Most librarians continue to operate in much the same way as when they started their careers. Working even harder to do more of what they are doing, they fail to do the new and different" (Matarazzo and Prusak 1997, 2). We also need to show vision and creativity. "Librarians should not engage in marketing the service as it is now" but as it *could* be (Seddon 1990, 35). To be a great marketer you must be flexible, be able to stand up for your strategy against those who disagree with it, be bold, be able to act quickly on new information, and know your facts. A good asset for a library marketer is an entrepreneurial spirit—a willingness to try new things and treat the library as a business (or a business within a business) whether it is for profit or not.

## WHAT TO MARKET?

When deciding what to market, you need to choose which of the many products and services that your library currently provides or could provide you want to emphasize. What products and services does your library provide right now? Of these, which do you deem successful (that is, used and valued)? Which have been failures—and why? Could these failures become successes with some relatively minor changes? What products and services could your library provide if there was funding or support for them? This is a good time for "blue-sky" thinking, that is, imagining what could be done if there were no barriers of time, money, or human resources.

Before you start examining specific products and services, it is worthwhile to look at what the *real* product of your library is. You do not provide books or journals or even document delivery or quick reference or online searches or bibliographies. You do not even provide information. A good library provides its customers with *answers* to their questions, with *solutions* to their problems. These are your real products.

### Know Thine Enemy: The Competition

"Competitors are those who anticipate customer demands and satisfy them before the librarians do. Anyone the customer perceives can meet these needs, whether the customer is correct or not, is a competitor" (Shamel 2002, 65). Who are your competitors? Why do your customers choose them over you? What do they do better or faster or cheaper than you? Can you compete with them and, if so, is it worth it to you? What would you have to give up (in time or other services) to compete? You cannot be complacent; even if you are your customers' first choice now, that situation can change any time. Many users go to the Internet first, but they don't realize that often the librarian played a major role in providing access to it. Peers and experts are also popular sources of information. This creates a wonderful opportunity for a proactive librarian to develop a database of the experts that your customers consult and market it to them.

Not only do our users have and use other sources, they also measure our libraries against them. Your competition may be the megabookstore (Borders, Barnes and Noble, W. H. Smith, and others). Does your library look as inviting or as well lit? Is it as conveniently located and easy to use? Are your clerks and librarians as friendly and as available? Is your facility clean and neat? Do you have comfortable chairs for your customers? Even academic libraries are not immune to competition. Students at most colleges and universities can and do conduct their own research on the Internet. The quality of the results might be questionable, but searching in the comfort of one's own dorm room is very seductive.

One kind of competition that you may not have thought of is what Deborah C. Sawyer (2002, 83) calls "left-field competition," a sudden and unforeseen change in the library's environment. For example, a sudden increase in demand for library services may encourage new competitors to enter the market, while a sudden drop may result in loss of income or profitability. Other examples are new requirements, such as service or availability twenty-four hours a day, seven days a week; availability of a new technology about which you know nothing; or a new standard or requirement that you must meet, such as a change in accreditation rules. The commoditization of information, wherein price, rather than service, becomes the deciding factor, has changed the way that many libraries must do business and introduced many potential competitors to the information services market.

Some competition comes from inside your own organization. Perhaps another group in the organization, less qualified than the library, has taken on the task of information delivery (usually because there was no library or the library was not marketed or its products and services were perceived as too expensive or inconvenient). Personal subscriptions to journals, books and manuals in private collections, or one's own network of colleagues also provide information competition for the library. In many organizations "end-users always bought certain classes of content like market research services and departmental subscriptions to trade journals. But the users had no skill sets and no understanding of how to properly utilize the collections or how to evaluate sources and credibility" (Stratigos in Pemberton 1999, 45). To make matters worse, some library vendors are even bypassing the library and going directly to our customers. On one occasion I found out that a library vendor was making a presentation to a department manager in the company in which I worked. I asked to be present. After the vendor finished his presentation, outlining all the wonderful things his very expensive service could provide, I simply told the manager, "I can do all that, at a fraction of the cost." The vendor did not make a sale, and that department's use of the library increased.

## Know Thine Friend: The Customer

As important as it is to know what you can provide, it is much more important to know what your customers need. "Just start out simple. Deliver what the user wants" (Pace 2000, 64). Some products may be used by your customers, but if they are not providing value, they are not important and should not be allocated too many of your scarce resources. For example, in a survey of my customers, the *Wall Street Journal* was the most used of my services but the least valued by the company. If I had cancelled the subscription, there would have been an outcry from my customers, but no harm would be done to the success of the corporation.

How do you find out what your customers need or want? Ask them! For too many years librarians have felt that they knew what was important for their users better than the users did. However, only the customer knows what his or her needs are, and only the customer (by using or not using the product or service) or the funder (by giving or withdrawing financial support) determines the value of the product or service. As essential as the customer is for information regarding his or her needs, remember that "customers are more than a source for data collection; they are the reason for libraries' existence" (Hernon and Altman 1998, xiv).

Needs are often assessed using A. H. Maslow's hierarchy (1943). The most basic human need is biological—food, shelter, and sleep. There is no direct library equivalent at this level. Security is the next level. In the library this would correspond to the way the library is organized, including the physical arrangement of books and tables and so forth, traffic flow, and even cataloging—whatever is necessary to produce an orderly and predictable environment for both the customer and the librarian. Personal safety and job security also fit at this level. Social needs are next—to belong to something, to have friends. For the customer this means the library staff is friendly, interested in what he or she wants or needs. For the library staff it also includes fitting into the institution or community's own culture, getting along with the other staff and the interpersonal networks they develop. The next to highest level of human needs is for esteem. For the customer this means being treated with respect, listened to, and valued. For the librarian, it includes being perceived as powerful and influential within the organization or community, being asked to present seminars, being seen as an expert, getting published, holding office in a professional or community organization, and receiving awards. The topmost level is self-actualization—becoming the best we can be. Helping our customers to meet their information needs, whether for work or personal development, is the basic mission of the library and represents this highest level of need fulfillment. For the staff, it means receiving recognition and praise from others, especially ones' peers and supervisors. For many people, money is not the ultimate reward—recognition is.

## The Six Ps of Marketing

Critical to the success of your marketing program is the right *product* at the right *price* in the right *place, promoted* in the right way to the right *people* at the right *point in time*. Let's look at each of these in turn.

### MARKETING P1: THE RIGHT PRODUCT

The library's product includes all materials in the library or available from other libraries or electronic sources (the Internet, remote databases, interlibrary loan) plus everything that is necessary to get the products to the client (acquisitions, cataloging and classification, online catalogs, the library website). It also includes all library services, both existing and potential (reference, story hour). Finally, the product also includes the staff of the library. "When it comes to offering a range of products within one entity, libraries can probably best be compared with shopping malls (no, I did not mean to say bookstores)" (Koontz 2002, 4). In larger libraries there are many departments (e.g., children's, reference, archives), but all are managed as a single unit—the library.

What is the difference between products and services? "Products are made; services are delivered. Products are used; services are experienced. Products possess physical characteristics we can evaluate before we buy; services do not even exist before we buy them. We request them, often paying in advance. Then we receive them, and finally, products are impersonal. . . . Services, by contrast, are personal" (Beckwith 2000, xvii). But marketing has to be backed up by more than just promises: "Even the best marketing in the world won't motivate a customer to purchase [use] a poor product or service more than once" (Levinson 1998, 12). Often we think that volume is the goal, and therefore the biggest must be the best. This is not true. Being number one in a small market (niche marketing) is often even better.

Products have a life cycle of introduction, growth, maturity, and decline. Innovation is important, but make sure you are introducing something that you do better than anyone else. However, "don't be too unique. Some folks develop products before considering whether those products solve real problems. If a product is too unique there might not be a market for it" (a marketing executive in Apelt 2001, 18). Before offering a new service, test it to make sure that you can meet the demand, that it works perfectly, and that it is priced to cover all costs. Assess its impact on the services you already provide. Also ask: Do I have the skills? Do I have the time? Do I have the resources? Is the service manageable? Can it be abused? (Hyman in Hernon and Whitman 2001, 157). You must be willing to discontinue a service as well. If its cost outweighs its benefits, if it is not central to the mission of the library or its parent organization or community, or if it doesn't fit in with other services, get rid of it. However, be aware that its customers may be dependent on it. You may want to make an alternative available (perhaps through an outside vendor). Decline can be postponed by changing the product slightly (eliminating some aspects, introducing new ones, and repackaging others), but eventually all products decline and disappear.

Prepackage your products, using a standardized package or brand so that it is obvious that the information came from the library. If you are purchasing some content from outside sources (document delivery, standards, research or market reports), make it appear as if it was your own by putting it in the same packaging as your other products. (This practice is called cobranding.) Make it easy for your customers to ask for standard statistics, current awareness searches, company financials or profiles. Create a catalog or product list. Have samples of each product type to hand to prospective customers. Company backgrounders can also be provided for salespeople in advance of their calling on a new (or even an existing) client and to those involved in mergers and acquisitions activity. Whether your catalog is card based or online, make it easy to find and access. Emphasize the value you add to it (subject headings) and the expertise needed to add that value. Make sure there is a link to your catalog on the institution or community's home page. Make the catalog attractive (look at the Web interfaces of amazon.com or barnes andnoble.com). Add reviews, graphics of book jackets, or enhanced search terms.

Marketing a service is different from marketing a product. A service is intangible; you cannot give free samples, and often even a free trial is not feasible. A service is inseparable from the person or persons providing it; your staff and their attitude are an integral part of the service. The customer is actively involved in the service. A service is inconsistent; not only can it vary from interaction to interaction, it is also not easily compared with services from competitors. A service is perishable; it has a short shelf life and cannot be stored. It is both offered and used at the same time and does not exist until the moment of service (Coote and Batchelor 1997). According to Peter Drucker (1985, 359), the performance of service institutions is measured by spending rather than action. Their agendas are controlled by others, whose priorities may even be in opposition to those of the service organization. These service institutions *must* do their job whether they have the resources or not.

## MARKETING *P*2: AT THE RIGHT PRICE

These days you must run your library like a business. This implies accountability, money management, and efficiency. This is good. It forces you to examine every aspect of the library to make sure that each is cost-effective.

> Those who hold the purse strings have become more cynical and want to see clearly that the money going into libraries is being spent well. The users (who ultimately determine value) are disconnected from the funders (who control the budget), and there is no one to make a direct value proposition for the library. Those doling out the organisational overhead dollars aren't necessarily library users and therefore have no basis for deciding if the return is worth the investment. Those information centres most likely to survive have a zero-based budget, meaning they charge back all their costs directly to users. This model is probably the most like running an independent business. In this scenario, there is no line-item for the intangible function known as "the library." It's more difficult for executives to conclude there's no value in their information spending if the users are paying for it at the point of need. (Strouse 2002, 48)

However, few charge back all of their costs; most are considered overhead.

Many librarians have a problem with pricing their products and services. The issue of free versus fee is still debated, not only in the public library sector, but also in corporate settings. "Many seem to think they have a right to free information, even when they intend to sell it on [to someone else] and make large sums of money themselves" (Hoey 1999, 49). Public library services aren't free; there is just no payment at time of service—services are prepaid. Even worse, as long as libraries are willing to give away their product, there will be those who think that their product is worth its price—nothing. "We tell all who will listen, 'library service is priceless,' then we price it low" (Scilken 1994, 10). For example, the auto club provides maps to its members at no cost but puts a price on the front. Customers should be made aware of the price of information—even if they are not charged.

No library will last long if its products and services lose money. If management requires you to cover your costs, make sure you know whether you are to include overhead costs such as space, light, heating, maintenance, and so on. Some libraries are even expected to be profit centers. Ask how much profit is acceptable to your management, community, or parent organization. Remember to include both direct and indirect costs and overhead. You may also want to have some kind of two-tier pricing, charging higher prices for high-demand items, rush service, or labor-intensive products or services. At the opposite end of the price spectrum is the loss leader. This involves setting an artificially low price on a product or service to attract business. Used with care this can be a good way to introduce an addition to your offerings. You can also use coupons, free samples, or discounts to market a new product or to emphasize an old one that is not being used as much as you would like. Beware of setting a low price just to undercut your competition, however. People who shop by price will leave you for a lower price.

Pricing is more an art than a science. Don't assume that logical pricing is smart pricing. "If no one complains about your price, it's too low. If almost everyone complains, it's too high" (Beckwith 1997, 132). You should aim for a price that causes about 20 percent of the customers to complain, remembering that 10 percent will complain about *any* price. You need to make your customers aware of why your products and services are priced as they are. There is the story of the carpenter called in to fix a squeaky floor. He took ten seconds to drive a nail and billed $42. When the home owner questioned the high cost for such a short time, the carpenter replied that the charge was $2 for the nail and $40 for knowing where to put it. "Don't charge by the hour. Charge by the years [of your experience]. Charge for knowing where" (Beckwith 1997, 138).

The final piece of the price puzzle is measuring the value of the library and its products and services. Value is "an amount considered to be a suitable equivalent [or exchange] for something else" (Olson 2002).

The exchange can involve money, a cost center number, taxes, or something else. "Value is added when library users are 'changed' for having library services and resources, allowing them to become more knowledgeable and empowered in decision making. Management and organizational culture need to realize this is the kind of value libraries can provide" (Weiner n.d.). Not all value can be expressed in monetary terms. Some may be qualitative or based on impact. Most benefits are based on users' best estimates or perceptions, which are notoriously hard to quantify.

To estimate library value, get as much cost data as you can. Collect as many user estimates of value as possible—on a continuing basis. Record as many impacts of the library as possible, both as specific monetary amounts and anecdotal data. Finally, analyze and determine cost-benefit ratios. José-Marie Griffiths and Donald W. King (1993, 150) found that the typical cost of a library consisted of salaries and benefits, 50 percent; space, 17 percent; equipment, 4 percent; services and supplies, 10 percent; and the collection, 19 percent. This mix may be changing. With the advent of so many services available on the Internet, I would think that the cost of services may be gaining on the cost of the collection. James M. Matarazzo and Laurence Prusak (1997, 8–9) asked how managers evaluate the library's value. Ten percent used time saved; 7 percent used money saved; 36 percent used internal surveys and other forms of feedback; 25 percent measured request volume and response time; and 7 percent used quality of information. Other major ways to measure a library's value are return on investment (ROI), cost-benefit analysis, and knowledge value added.

Each kind of library has its own kind of intangible benefits. For hospitals it may be avoiding unnecessary admissions or tests; in academia, renewed accreditation, higher rankings, or attracting endowments; in public libraries, contributing to the productivity of local government, the economic value of salaries from businesses attracted to the area, reducing the community's cost of information, or freeing money for other spending in the area (Cram 1995); or in corporate libraries, the creation of intellectual property in the form of patents or inventions.

In 2002 in St. Paul, Minnesota, the Department of Transportation (MN/DOT) was reorganizing, and, according to Jerry Baldwin (2002, 9), "any unit within the department that didn't deliver the product (construction projects) or directly support those units that did was looked at as a source of staff and monies that could be diverted. As always in difficult times, research, including MN/DOT Library, was one of the first areas looked at for potential savings." To stave off the library's closing, the staff reorganized to become stronger, pulling together facts and figures to prove that not only did it support the construction projects, but it saved money. As shown in figure 2-1, the MN/DOT Library "provided an estimated total of $8,386,500 in reduced costs and added value for a benefit-to-cost ratio of 12:1." As a result of the analysis, the library was saved.

## MARKETING *P*3: IN THE RIGHT PLACE

Even if you have the right product, it won't be successful if it doesn't get to the people who need it. People, as a rule, come to you, so location is important. For example, the renowned Enoch Pratt Library has been located in downtown Baltimore for years. It used to be surrounded by homes and businesses. However, today few people live nearby, and the business district is elsewhere. Their customers have left. How does the library reach them now? They go where the customers are. The Pratt has developed a twenty-four-hour phone-reference service; they reach the customers in their homes via telephone. In addition, the library has arranged to bus students to the library. A website is also a good way to

| Source | Savings |
|---|---|
| 4,500 information resources (document delivery) | $   191,250 |
| 3,600 requests for information on specific topics | $   468,000 |
| Centralized journals and routing | $   180,000 |
| Employees' reading of above documents and searches | $5,100,000 |
| Employees' reading of journals | $2,400,000 |
| Use of library Web pages | $     47,250 |

*Return on Investment (ROI)*
($839,250 savings and avoided costs + $7,547,250 value added) = $8,386,500 total benefits - $700,000 library costs (salaries, supplies, equipment, space) = ROI of $7,686,5500

*Cost-Benefit Ratio*
($839,250 savings and avoided costs + $7,547,250 value added)/($8,386,500 total benefits - $700,000 library costs) = benefit-to-cost ratio of 12:1 (Baldwin 2002, 11)

**FIGURE 2-1   Minnesota Department of Transportation Library Savings**

get the library to the right place—if it is a useful and up-to-date website and if it is promoted properly. However, you still have to get the word out to your customers that (1) there is a website and (2) that the website can answer their information needs.

Delivery is becoming more important in the age of the international organization. (Remember, not only corporations are international these days. Many nonprofits and universities have branches overseas.) The challenge of serving users around the globe is a daunting one, but the Internet can go a long way toward meeting it. Customers can e-mail document requests and, in some cases, receive the document as an e-mail attachment (or via fax) almost immediately. Reference questions come to the library by e-mail, and librarians can even conduct reference interviews via e-mail. After a search is conducted, the results can also be transmitted via e-mail. Another way to serve customers in other locations is by cooperation among librarians in various institutional locations. If a customer in New York needs some information at midnight and the New York library is closed, he or she can e-mail or call the Tokyo office, which is likely to be open. After the Tokyo office has taken care of the request, staff can send a copy of the results to the customer's home library in New York for follow-up.

You must deliver information in the way that your customers prefer. Does your client want the results delivered in person, by mail, by fax, over the phone, or via the Internet? What format does he or she want? Paper, a computer file (MS Word or plain text? Mac or PC?), a database, a spreadsheet, or a PowerPoint presentation? What information should be included? A list of bibliographic citations, summaries, or complete documents? Should the information be arranged with the best information first or in chronological order? How much does he or she need? Just one article or everything you've found on the subject? Should the information be in English or another language? Does the customer want raw data, tables, graphs, or your analysis? Are you expected to prepare a full report or just an executive summary?

## MARKETING *P*4: PROMOTED IN THE RIGHT WAY

Your marketing must present the right image. "Rather than soliciting more business, your public relations campaign can enhance your image and help maintain a positive presence within your organization" (Olson 2002). And, as Herbert S. White points out, you can help build the image you want: "What we need to tell people is not how wonderful our public libraries *are* but rather how wonderful they *could be*" (in Besant and Sharp 2000, 18, emphasis mine).

A key component of your marketing must be emphasizing the benefits of your products and services. You need to get inside the mind of your customers and look at your products and services from their points of view. What benefits might your customers want? Although a salesperson might want quick answers to win a crucial order, the president of an organization interested in expansion may want something quite different. Don't be afraid to be unconventional or to try something new. What worked in the past may not work today. What research says may not apply in your particular situation. What you "know" about your business and your customers may not really be true. What the "experts" say may just plain be wrong.

Look at what your library does better than the competition, and let your customers know. "Your service or product is not differentiated until the customer understands the difference" (Peters in Evans Ward, and Ruggas 2000, 89). That you are on-site and in-house are big pluses, as is your ability to tailor the collection to your user community. No outsider could possibly know as much about your customers as does your staff.

## MARKETING *P*5: TO THE RIGHT PEOPLE

This is the least visible *P* but perhaps the most important. To succeed, you need to make relationships with customers instead of just selling things. Customers are people, and with people, perception is more important than reality. "Customer expectations can influence satisfaction with both content and context. These expectations may or may not match what the library thinks appropriate, but nevertheless they represent reality for the consumer" (Hernon and Altman 1998, 8). The perceptions of the library's service personality by the users and the staff need to agree. If there is a big difference in the values and expectations of the library staff and those of the customers, the staff will be frustrated and the customers dissatisfied. They cannot tell if you did a good search. Therefore, you have to tell them. Feelings are important. Often when asked why he deals with a certain vendor, the customer says, "I like them" or "I feel comfortable with them" (Beckwith 1997). "Non-product and non-price considerations can carry as much as 70% of weight in purchase decisions" (Olson 2002). To win or keep your customers, you need to make your product or service more appealing and more accessible, the price more appealing, and your promotion more visible and persuasive (Hiam 2000, 12). "It is the customer's or client's emotional experience of the relationship that weighs most heavily on how they go about selecting a supplier. The mere existence of a prior relationship may be enough to preclude consideration of any other options" (Sawyer 2002, 24). The cost of changing service providers, measured in time, distance to travel, learning the ins and outs of the new vendor's system, and so on, may outweigh any benefits, especially monetary benefits. "Advertise your successes"—that you beat their deadline, came in under budget, helped them make a sale, or otherwise contributed to the success of your client (Beckwith 1997, 225–26).

Because the customer is paramount, you must know as much about your current and prospective customers as possible. Ask yourself: Who are my customers? For what do they use my library? Are they aware of all the services provided? Do I have the right balance between print and electronic service delivery? Do they get what they want? Are they treated in the way they want to be treated? How do I collect and use customer feedback? How do I introduce my library to new staff? What training is available for library staff? What training does my library provide for its customers? What is my library's Web or intranet presence? How does this relate to my organization's Web or intranet presence? What is my competitive advantage? Stephen Abram suggests you ask your customers some questions, too: "What keeps you awake at night? If you could solve only one problem (at work), what would it be? If you could change one thing and one thing only, what would it be?" (in Hane 2002, 35).

You also need to know how information flows within the organization or community. There are many ways of sharing information and knowledge: person-to-person, in writing, via the computer. Which medium is chosen is a function of the nature of the data, personal preferences, urgency, and available communication tools. How fast do your customers usually need a response? These days "users expect to have their research needs met instantaneously via the computer" (Adams and Cassner 2001, 6). What are their information-handling skills? What do they want now? What will they want in the future?

Who will be the target of your marketing? Will it be your primary users, those who fund your library, the community in general, new users, or users who have quit coming to the library? "The answers you had when you started in business may be different today and in the twenty-first century" (Levinson 1998, 36). You don't have to limit yourself to just one target. In fact, most libraries have multiple constituencies and should market to all of them at one time or another. Academic libraries may promote to the administration, the faculty (especially new faculty), nonacademic staff, students, and even the public. Libraries in associations and other not-for-profit institutions may target their members and staff, some of the public, journalists, and other librarians. The users of law libraries are lawyers, paraprofessionals, court staff, journalists, other librarians, students (law and others), and maybe even the public (especially for county or court libraries). Medical libraries serve physicians, nurses, students, staff, patients, and occasionally the public. Libraries in government agencies are used by in-house staff, the public, and other librarians. It is also important to "find out what your clients *don't* like or need and stop doing it" (Bell 1998, 7, emphasis mine).

There are many ways to find out what users want, need, or value. Surveys or questionnaires provide only aggregate data and do not go into enough detail so are the least useful, but they are also the easiest and cheapest methods. Here are examples of questions you might want to include. Describe some of the typical duties of your job. Which library services do you actually use—and how often? In what subject area are you most interested? (You may want to list the areas about which you would like feedback and have them check them off or rank them.) What kind of books do you read regularly? What information sources do you regularly consult or have at your desk (or in your home)? Do you refer others to the library? Why or why not? If you don't use the library, where do you go? Why? For what kinds of information and for what purposes? Are these other sources satisfactory? Why or why not? Think back to a recent time when you needed information. What information did you need? For what purpose? How did you find it? Was it enough? How successful are you usually in finding information? How often do you not even look for information—or go to the library—because you either thought you wouldn't find it or it would be too much trouble or cost too much? What sort of frustrations and time delays are you encountering in finding information? What one thing could the library do—or improve—that would help you most? How will we know we're doing a good job, in your eyes? What would be your reaction to the library adding a user-friendly service that would allow library users to do their own computer literature searches? Do you request an analysis of the retrieved information by the librarian? Does giving your research problems to the librarians save you time?

Focus groups can be useful but require even more expertise, and as we all know, it's not focus groups who buy products, but people. Observation is a great way to find out what people use but cannot give an idea of what people need or value. Interviews are the best way to get useful information, but they are time-consuming and require training and experience to conduct properly. However, quality information is what you need, and interviews remain the best way to obtain this information. Finally, combine two or more methods or questions to validate the answers, a process called *triangulation*. A good technique is to use a survey first, to help determine the major areas of interest and concern in your organization or community. Then conduct in-depth interviews with selected members of the organization and management or community and board. Don't forget to include people who are not library users. Ask them why they don't use the library. Perhaps they don't know it exists or what it can do for them, or it isn't open (or not staffed) when they need it. If they think that they don't need the library, they just may not know what their own needs are. Do they think that the library doesn't have what they need, prefer your competition (for reasons you had better understand), or think that your cost is too high or value is too low? (Remember, in many cases user cost is measured in terms of time rather than money.) Have the nonusers encountered problems with service or staff in the past that have turned them off of the library?

A great deal of library literature deals with the information audit or the information-needs analysis. A needs analysis is often done for a library that may or may not yet exist, asks simple questions, is a reactive technique, seeks definite or specific responses, and can easily be conducted by in-house staff. The information audit is used to evaluate current information services, asks both subjective and objective questions, is more proactive, seeks trends and concepts among users and nonusers, and is best done by outside consultants in conjunction with in-house staff.

Let's look first at the information audit. It identifies information required by the organization, information currently supplied (by the library and others), gaps, inconsistencies and duplications, information flows in the organization and from outside (and *to* the outside), and provides "strategic direction for management of the organization's information resources and development of a formal information policy" (Henczel 2001, xxii). "An information audit can also reveal time and money wasted on information sources that no one uses and show why no one uses them" (Dobson 2002, 32). There are seven stages in an information audit: (1) planning, (2) collecting data, (3) analyzing data, (4) evaluating data, (5) communicating recommendations, (6) implementing recommendations, and (7) gathering feedback on the above on an ongoing basis, measuring changes and effects of the audit (Henczel 2001, 17).

The customer information-needs analysis (CINA) does not look at how users use the library but at their needs. "In information-needs analysis, an understanding of the users' goals is often as useful as the identification of specific needs" (Westbrook 2001, 7). You can conduct a needs analysis to support budgeting, prioritizing, positioning, allocating resources, planning for change, visioning, or marketing. A hidden benefit of the process is that it creates a relationship that builds trust as you find out more about your customers. You can use this information to anticipate their needs by knowing what similar customers have chosen. This technique is used to good effect by Web merchants such as amazon.com and Barnes and Noble when they suggest other materials in which the customer may be interested. When interpreting the CINA, it is important to remember that "not all needs should or can be met" (Westbrook 2001, 7), so you will need to work to identify those needs that are consistent with your library's goals.

Chris Dobson prefers to call this process an "information checkup" that can identify information problems early (2002, 32). The first step is to define the goal of or purpose for the checkup. Is library traffic down? Do you need background for collection development? Are some products or services not "selling"? Are you looking for input to your strategic plan? Is there a budget battle coming up? Are you trying to benchmark your library against others? "Although you may want to, you can't get the answer to every question in your first checkup" (Dobson 2002, 33). Write down everything that you want to ask; then rank these questions. Ask only "big" questions. Instead of asking, "Should we get ProQuest [or any other specific service]?" ask, "What types of information do you need?" and "What problems do you have using electronic databases?" Then get management support for the project. "Put your goals in terms management understands. 'Guidance for collection development' may become 'a study to insure that resources are expanded for the areas of greatest need and potential return on investment'" (Dobson 2002, 33). Next, hire a consultant and develop a budget. "Even if a consultant only confirms what you know, the consultant's opinion will carry more weight than yours. Somehow the act of paying for advice and opinions imbues them with tremendous validity" (Dobson 2002, 33). The final step is to gather the information. One benefit of interviews is that they allow us to look beyond initial reactions. For instance, perhaps a former customer experienced document delivery that was too slow for his need. Now you can deliver most documents in less than twenty-four hours. During an interview you can let him know of the improvement and perhaps win him back as a customer. Include the highest level of management you can get to cooperate.

Use customer information to personalize what you supply to them. "The future of information provision is surely personalised information flows" (Nicholas 2000, 16). The personal touch, such as a handwritten note from the library director, a personal invitation to a library program, or a note telling a customer about a new book on a favorite topic or by a favorite author, is what your customers will appreciate most, and the more frequent the customer receives such personal touches, the better. Have you thought of establishing a frequent-user or frequent-searcher club? Perhaps you could give users a free search after ten searches or after a certain dollar amount is spent. Or free admission to a library program after a certain number of items are checked out. The possibilities are intriguing.

Another people issue is that of customer training (what used to be called "bibliographic instruction"). "We know lots of stuff our patrons don't, and sometimes they don't even know enough to know they need our expertise" (Shear 2001, 14). We used to think we were supposed to teach our patrons to find information on their own, especially in academia. Now we are afraid our customers won't need us because they can find information on their own. It is important to teach them what is *not* there. A customer once came to me after spending an hour on the Web looking for a price list for one of our competitors. I knew that it wasn't there. I asked him if our company put its price list on the Web. He replied, "Of course not." So why would he expect our competitors to do so? He would not have wasted that hour if he had just contacted me before he searched. Fortunately, not all of our customers are so ignorant of our value. Joan Shear found that "the most frequent users of reference service are often the most skilled researchers—perhaps because they are doing the most complicated research, but maybe because they know enough about research to realize that there are all sorts of tools and techniques they haven't learned yet. And they know that we, as professional librarians, may just have something to teach them" (2001, 14).

Satisfying the information needs of managers and executives is a challenge for many librarians, whether in a for-profit situation or not. Because a major issue for managers is time, the ability to respond rapidly is one of the library's competitive advantages and should be emphasized in marketing to this group. Don't waste their time with long reports. Make sure that they are timely, well organized (with comparisons to previous years or the budget), easy to review, reliable, and accurate (McKinnon and Bruns 1992, 132).

To maximize your marketing efforts, you should realize that your market is made up of different segments. You can divide customers geographically (for instance, urban versus rural, zip code, department); demographically (age, income, occupation, ethnicity, sex, education, religion); behaviorally (user or nonuser, why they use the library); or psychologically (lifestyle, computer experience, social class, personality).

## MARKETING *P*6: AT THE RIGHT POINT IN TIME

Marketing the right product at the wrong time is a waste of time. The wrong time can be either too early (before the customer knows he or she needs the product) or too late (after he or she has already bought from someone else). Yet when the product is the information center and the services librarians can offer, there really is no wrong time for marketing.

## WHEN TO MARKET?

If you're wondering when to market, the answer is easy—always. Every encounter with a customer or a prospective customer is a marketing opportunity. "As information professionals, it is easy to sit at the reference desk and wait for the next customer to walk up and ask a question. It's a trap that can lead to the demise of a library in the corporate [or any other] world" (Swart 2000). Market at the time of need, when a customer has already shown interest, by coming to you for assistance. He or she will be more receptive to your marketing message. And you can't just market once. The marketplace changes, with competitors— and customers—coming and going. You've heard the phrase "you're only as good as your last sale"? The library is only as good as the last time a customer was served. No matter how satisfied he or she may be, a customer will forget about you if you don't remind him or her that (1) you exist and (2) how much you can help with his or her business, hobby, or problem. Continual marketing gives you an advantage over any competitors who do not do the same. Finally, each marketing campaign allows you to build on the investment (in time, money, or ideas) you've already made both in marketing and in the customer. "Scattershot marketing wastes money and time" (Apelt 2001, 17). Marketing and service should be like zero-based budgeting; each campaign should start at the beginning, with looking at your services and your customers. Never assume that what worked last time will work again. Is the service or product still viable or still priced right?

Marketing is not just the responsibility of the library manager or those staff who interact with the customers. Everyone, even cataloging, acquisitions, book processing, janitors, and delivery persons, must constantly keep in mind that the ultimate object of his or her activities is satisfying the customer. One marketing technique is cross-selling. When you provide a customer with one product or service, mention a complementary product or service that he or she might be able to use. For instance, along with the results of an online search, send the proper form for requesting an interlibrary loan or another form of document delivery, or follow the delivery of a book that the customer has requested with a list of other books in the collection on the same subject. (In a large library you might just send a note saying, "If this book is useful to you, similar books will be found under the following call numbers . . .")

I am sure that other marketing opportunities will become apparent to you once you start thinking in terms of cross-selling. In fact, you will start looking for such marketing opportunities.

## WHERE TO MARKET?

Your first priority in marketing should be to customers and potential customers within your own institution or community.

> Market yourself to those who can afford to support the library. Not only do you want them to use your services, but also you want—and need—their financial support. Market to those who use your library but who cannot afford to support the library. Likely this group needs the library and its services, since the library can—depending on the library's charter—give this group some services for free. And perhaps one day this group will be able to support you, so it is important that they remember you. Market to those who can afford to support the library, but do not use your services. You have resources to offer them and perhaps they have support they can give you. Market to those who cannot afford to support the library and who do not use your services. They need you and if they become successful, they should be able to support the library—hopefully in acknowledgement for the support you gave them. (Hurst 2001a, 6)

In for-profit institutions, downplay the soft benefits of your services and products (time savings, efficiency, collaboration, and so forth) and emphasize the hard benefits (for instance, money saved, time to market cut, reduction of head count, avoidance of increased insurance costs, fewer unnecessary hospital tests or admissions). Be sure that you have hard data to support any claims you make—they are very likely to ask for them. Your presentations or materials should be short, to the point, and written using no library jargon. The use of business jargon, on the other hand, is very desirable. Including current business buzzwords shows that you are up-to-date.

Some special librarians also market their services and products to customers outside their institution. One potential market is your organization's own customers. You could repackage online searches done for internal customers and sell them as bibliographies or information packets to outside customers. You could even include synopses or analyses or even copies of the documents listed. (Be sure to secure permission from the copyright holders, including the search service and database producers.) Hospital and law firm libraries might offer their online search services and document delivery to outside physicians or attorneys for a fee. One advantage to offering services to outside customers is that the library can move from being a cost center to a profit center. This alone could improve the library's ability to withstand downsizing or elimination in an economic crunch. In addition, providing excellent service to an institution's own customers helps to improve the image of the institution, which will enhance the library's own image and position within the organization.

## HOW TO MARKET?

Marketing is not hard. I'll say that again. Marketing is not hard. It just takes organization and some good ideas. You'll have to do the organizing, but here are a lot of good ideas. Not all will work in your particular library, but you should be able to use at least a few.

### Ranganathan and Marketing

S. R. Ranganathan's "Five Laws of Librarianship" can be applied to library marketing (Jain et al. 1999, 6).

> *First law:* "Books are for use." (Maximize the use of books.)
>
> *Second law:* "Every reader his book." (The reader is the prime factor, and his or her needs must be satisfied.)
>
> *Third law:* "Every book its reader." (Find a reader for every book.)
>
> *Fourth law:* "Save the time of the reader." (Organize information in such a way that the reader finds the wanted information promptly.)
>
> *Fifth law:* "A library is a growing organism." (Emphasize comprehensive and evolutionary growth.)

If you substitute *library resources* for *books* and *customer* for *reader,* you have the beginnings of a basic library marketing plan.

#### LIBRARY RESOURCES ARE FOR USE

Implicit in Ranganathan's first law is that if a resource is not being used, it should be either eliminated or marketed. Look at the services you think are being underutilized. Are they really necessary to your customers? If they are not, then eliminate them. Nearly every library does some things just because "they've always been done." I've even heard of librarians writing reports that no one reads. If you discontinue a service and find that your customers cry out for it, you can always reinstate it. If no one objects, it is confirmation that the service wasn't needed in the first place. What if a service or product that you feel is one of your best is not being used enough to justify its continuation? You can change it; add something, delete something, repackage it. Then reposition it in the minds of your customers. Market it as a new product with the focus on what is changed. Expand existing services to new clients. Sell new services that are just one step beyond current ones you have now. Disaggregate some services and repackage each as a new service.

The era of acquiring books "just in case" they might be needed is over. Most libraries now use the "just-in-time" acquisition theory (except for large research libraries, and even they are changing). Weed out books that are not being checked out or consulted in-house. If someone asks for a book that you have discarded, you can always borrow it from another library. Just as you should discontinue unnecessary services, remember to market *all* the services that you keep. Too often we only market what is physically in the library. Don't forget to tell your customers about all the information sources that you have access to through the Internet, interlibrary loan, reciprocal borrowing privileges with other libraries, and networking with other librarians. Feature services available through the library website, but don't make the mistake of giving the impression that customers will never have to come to the library. You have to be proactive. The current ALA campaign, "@ Your Library," "takes an essentially passive stance: we have something you might like, stop by if you have the time" (Sass 2002, 38). You must encourage or even urge your customers to use your services. Make it seem like they couldn't possibly do their jobs effectively without your services.

## EVERY CUSTOMER HIS OR HER LIBRARY RESOURCES

You must have, provide, and market what your customers need. Go beyond user surveys.

> Could you visit every area in your organization? Could you visit every area locally? Could you send an email to each department head or to every administrative assistant briefly introducing the services of the library? Could you send notes of congratulations,

perhaps to mark a person's anniversary date with the organization or a job well done? Could you attend the department meetings of other departments (with permission of that department)? Not only would this give you an opportunity to meet the people in that department, but you would also be able to hear firsthand the issues, concerns and project areas of that department. Could you visit with or call every new employee? New employees often want to meet other employees in order to learn more about the organization they have joined. Imagine if you were one of the people who reached out to them? Not only would they know who you were, but also they would think very positively of you and the library because you dared to reach out to them. Could you call every employee and ask how the library could help them? Although this sounds daunting, what if you began by calling your clients. During those conversations you could ask who else in their departments should be using the library and then call those people. This would be what is called a "warm call" (versus a "cold call") because you can tell them that you were referred to them, and that other person's name hopefully will "warm" the way. Instead of sending promotional material about the library through interoffice mail to everyone, could you stand at the entrance in the morning and personally hand the literature to employees as they arrived? This would put a face on the library. (Hurst 2001a, 7)

However, it is not enough to make customers happy. We must "delight" them. Do more than they expect. According to Harry Beckwith, "Don't just create what the market needs or wants. Create what it would *love*" (1997, 20, emphasis mine). For example, in a public library, add comic books for teens; provide city maps and travel information in a corporate library; provide continuing legal or medical education materials in law or hospital libraries. Make a file of user preferences, for example, wants all citations, only wants summaries, needs large print, likes mysteries, reads French but not German, and so forth. You can keep this file on cards or on the computer, but refer to it whenever you deal with the customer. Customization is knowing what the customer wants and giving it to him or her. Mass customization is incorporating this into the business routine, doing it *all* the time for *all* the customers (Peppers and Rogers 1997). Every time you have something new or different in your library, let your customers know. Write a newsletter, post a sign, take out an ad, send out a flier, incorporate it into your voice-mail message or e-mail signature—but get the word out!

## EVERY LIBRARY RESOURCE ITS CUSTOMER

Every resource occupies a position in the mind of the customer. Al Ries and Jack Trout (1981, 193-200) provide some questions to ask about positioning. I have added some examples from libraryland.

1. What position do you own? (books, old, stodgy, boring, behind the curve)
2. What position do you want to own? (up-to-date, forward thinking, a leader, answers, solutions)
3. Whom must you outgun? (information technology staff, the Internet, colleagues)
4. Do you have enough money? (Can you get enough support from management or the board, your staff?)
5. Can you stick it out? (Are you willing to take the risk of it not working? What if you fail?)
6. Do you match your position? (Are you creative, daring? Can you meet the expectations you will raise?)

"Position is a passive noun: it's something the market does to you" (Beckwith 1997, 112). It's not where *you* think you are that matters; it's where *they* think you are. However, you can change that with marketing. Find the hardest job in your area (or the most difficult area for your customers), and position yourself as the expert in it. This will give you a strong competitive advantage over other providers of information (your competitors). It is no longer possible to know everything about everything and to provide everything to everyone. "Having a focus can improve a company's quality perception in the [customer's] mind in four separate ways."

1. The specialist effect: "Everybody knows a specialist knows more about his or her specialty than a general practitioner does. Whether it's true or not doesn't really matter. The perception is reality."
2. The leadership effect: "Leadership alone is the most powerful driver a business can own." The leader must be the best. The leader tends to stay the leader.
3. The price effect: the more expensive it is, the better it must be. "A high price is not a negative."
4. The name effect: "The most distinguishing characteristic of a good (or bad) name is its sound" (Ries 1996, 90–93).

Jack Trout and Steve Rivkin (1996) suggest positioning yourself (or your library) as synonymous with one concept only. Xerox means copying, FedEx "owns" the idea of overnight delivery, and Scotch equals tape. Even though you're good at a lot of things, focus on one thing at a time; otherwise, you run the risk of either confusing your customers or diluting the impact of the marketing program. Mount another campaign at another time to focus on another product or service. "After you say one thing, repeat it again and again" (Beckwith 1997, 175).

Don't lose focus by getting away from the product or service that made you great. If your reputation was built on excellent online searching, don't suddenly decide that your customers should do their own searches. By abandoning your strongest service, you weaken the perception of your value. Another way to lose focus is by adding too many new products or services. If you aren't good at something (like document delivery), don't do it; do only what you can do excellently. You can also lose focus by going outside your geographic area. Is a great local library going to be a great national (or regional) one? Not likely. Moving into other geographic (or cultural) areas is fraught with risk. Do you understand the new culture?

If your library is small, don't apologize or try to hide your size. Make smallness your advantage. This is especially true of one-person libraries. Because the solo librarian does everything, he or she gets to know the customers and their needs and preferences especially well. He or she is perfectly placed to provide very personalized service and to be very responsive to changes in the organization or community's situation.

Repositioning is the process of moving from an old position or perception to a newer, next-generation place. If you had to identify your library with one word, what word would that be? Many of our customers would say *books*, but we are so much more than that. Some librarians would say *service*, but that is not bold enough. How about *information*? That's better, broader, and more inclusive of all the various media and resources available. Unfortunately, the computer people have co-opted this word, and that is not where we want to be positioned. I strongly feel that the best one-word description of a library should be either *answers* or *solutions*. After all, that is what our customers have really come in for—answers to their questions, solutions to their problems. That is the position we seek in their minds. Perhaps you have been seen as the best library for business reference. Then you branched out into fee-for-service, Internet instruction, and some other areas. However, these weren't all that successful. Now your customers wonder about the quality of your business reference. It is time to position your library as *the* expert in business reference once again. Either drop the new and unsuccessful services or rebrand them under, perhaps, the fee-for-service division, and commit that division to becoming the best in its niche. This situation could have been avoided by using a new brand for the new services in the first place. An example from business: *Levi* was synonymous with *denim*. When they added upscale pants, they created the Dockers brand. Both lines sold well.

Moya Lum (2000, 12) described repositioning the AMP library: "As of November 1998, AMP's Information and Library Services (ILS) ceased to exist. From its ashes rose the AMP Corporate Research Centre." A knowledge management officer was added to the staff. "We have positioned ourselves as consultants and *solution providers* in the area of information and knowledge management, database design and development" (emphasis mine). Lum points out that the center and staff do not "wait until we are asked to prove our value but go out to demonstrate it constantly in our interactions with senior management." They credit constant improvement, flexibility of staff, and "the willingness to let go of outmoded ways of operating" for their survival. "We never forget that our primary purpose as a special library is to respond to the needs of our parent organisation."

Another way to market your resources is branding. Most libraries do not have a brand—a consistent image or style. Branding is how you can make your name and identity recognizable. A brand, in the customer's mind, is a warranty, a promise of performance. The customer may think, "If it comes from the library, it must be good." (An unfortunate brand "warranty" is the Internet, where people often think that "if it is on the Net, it must be right.") A brand identifies products (and services) with their source—your library. Making everything that comes from the library have a similar look and feel not only looks good, but "this also makes us look savvy" (Chochrek 2000, 34). Make sure that everything leaving the library has at least the name, phone number, and URL of the library on it. If you have a motto, slogan, symbol, mascot, or other graphic, be sure to use it on everything.

## SAVE THE TIME OF THE CUSTOMER

The most common benefit claimed by librarians is that we can do it better, cheaper, and faster, what I call the librarian's mantra. Better is subjective, cheaper is often irrelevant because most libraries do not charge (directly) for their services and products, but faster is a measurable benefit. "Faster is no longer enough. The search for the instantaneous and simultaneous has become the 1990s equivalent of the quest for the Holy Grail" (McKenna 1997, 1). Regis McKenna wrote, "Real time is characterized by the shortest possible lapse between idea and action; between initiation and result. In the context of business, a real time

## CASE STUDY

### PRESCRIPTION FOR SUCCESSFUL MARKETING
### Sidney Liswood Library,
### Mount Sinai Hospital, Toronto, Ontario, Canada

Sandra Kendall had been on the job one year. "Now it seemed like a good time for an 'annual checkup.' Our resources, library services, and staff skill sets were fulfilling the baseline for a small hospital library. But how could we be better? How could we increase our visibility within the hospital?" (Kendall and Massarella 2001, 29). She went to each chief of service to find out what he or she wanted from the library. She was surprised to learn that the users were not aware of many of the library's new acquisitions. "It became clear to me that our users needed to be reintroduced to our updated skills and services. For this hospital library to be repositioned, we had to develop a deliberate strategy for success" (30). Kendall and her staff started by redesigning the library space to make it more customer-friendly. By partnering with another department, they were able to create a computer learning lab in a corner of the library reading room without having to pay for the computer equipment. They announced the remodeling with an article in the hospital newsletter, complete with testimonials from regular library users from various hospital departments and a sidebar highlighting features of the intranet.

The librarian also found that the nursing department used the library heavily without the appropriate support materials. Nursing reference questions, training sessions, and interlibrary loans were a growing percentage of library usage. Kendall drafted a collection development proposal for the nursing department that included creation of a specific nursing intranet site. She received funding to improve the collection, with the proviso that the library would market the collection and offer training on how to use the nursing resources. "When it was ready, we put an 'e-nursing' button on the library intranet to direct nurses right to 'their' section" (Kendall and Massarella 2001, 30). She and a nurse go to each nursing station to announce and demonstrate the new e-nursing site. "By going to the nurses in their work areas and at the same time respecting their work with the patients and adjusting our presentations accordingly, we emphasized that e-nursing is a tool designed to work for the nurses" (31).

Since beginning this repositioning plan, the library has gained more staff and a 50 percent increase in budget. "We've been inundated with requests from other departments to create focused sites for them akin to e-nursing, so we've begun an organized process of adding client-driven one-stop buttons to our intranet site." They now present information on their intranet services at employee orientation, rather than a tour of the library, and have been added to the intern orientation program. "The Sidney Liswood Library is seen as a content provider rather than a physical space" (Kendall and Massarella 2001, 32).

experience is created from self-service and self-satisfaction by customers. It is an instant response" (6). In the library this is exactly what our customers expect and demand. Libraries with multiple offices worldwide can do this. Public libraries with employees working shifts covering twenty-hours a day can do it, too. Smaller libraries can create a virtual reference desk via the Web or voice mail or e-mail. Perhaps the answer won't come back immediately, but the request can be transmitted whenever the requester thinks of it, and the librarian can respond whenever he or she has the answer. Another practical solution is the creation of library FAQs (frequently asked question lists) on the Web or posting answers to past requests, enabling the customer to solve the problem on his or her own. Finally, how about setting up electronic discussion lists or expert networks so that customers can request information from other customers within their own organization or community, thereby extending the library's expertise?

Saving time is obvious in the case of document delivery. It should also be obvious in the case of searching, especially on the Web. We know that we can find things faster because (1) we know where to look, (2) we know how to look, and (3) we know when not to use the Web at all. Some of our time-savers are less obvious. By teaching our customers how better to use the resources in the library or at their desktops or computers, we save them time in finding answers. Provide instruction on how each resource works, which ones are best for which questions, and a few tips and tricks for better retrieval. Most users don't even know that in most Web search engines you should enclose a phrase in quotation marks. This one tip can save users a tremendous amount of time. Imagine how much time you can save if you arrange for a training session on a heavily used database, such as Engineering Index for a group of engineers or Humanities Index in a public library. Most likely, it will cost you nothing and will almost certainly boost the library's image in the minds of its users (and, therefore, in the eyes of those who fund the library). Do your customers waste time wandering around the library looking for what they need? Or are you and your staff always answering "Where is . . .?" questions? If the answer is yes, perhaps you need to look at your signage. It always amazes me how few signs there are in libraries and how poorly placed they are. Also, examine the places where staff and customers interact—the circulation desk, the information kiosk, the reference desk—and examine your business cards and brochures. Are they obvious, easy to find or read, friendly, and current? "Then ask: what are we doing to make a *phenomenal* impression at every point?" Then "improve each one—*significantly*" (Beckwith 1997, 51).

## A LIBRARY IS A GROWING ORGANISM

The one constant in the life of a library is that nothing is constant. Our products and services must keep up with these changes. "Make sure you keep coming up with new ideas and rotate services, so your information never seems stale. Keep a short list of services that don't change" (Chochrek 2000, 33). Constantly survey your customers to determine if and how their needs have changed. Make it easy for your customers to tell you what you did well and what was done poorly. Attach a customer feedback card to everything that goes out (or to random items). Minimize the amount of information he or she needs to enter. Fill in the customer's name, department, and date. Put the return address of the library on the reverse of the card so the customer can just put it in the mail. (If you are sending it out by post, prepaying the return postage will make it much more likely that the card will be returned.) Figure 2-2 is a sample of a customer feedback form that can be mailed to customers. Check boxes get a better response than fill-in-the-blank questions. Be sure to add a section called "Other Comments" to capture additional information and the occasional compliment.

Another response form might be placed on the circulation desk or, better, handed to each customer as he or she leaves the library. Figure 2-3 is a sample of an in-house customer feedback form.

If a product or service is not working, do something about it before your competition makes it a complete failure and taints your hard-won image as a leader. Then come up with something completely new. To use the example above of the library with the great reference service, how about a virtual answer center? Give the new service a new name—say, "Answers at Your Fingertips."

### Creative Marketing

All kinds of marketing need imagination and creativity. There is no "magic formula" into which you can plug data and receive answers. Jay Conrad Levinson suggests several ways to increase your marketing creativity (1998, 50–52). Figure out one product or service that will excite your customers and focus on that. Next, "translate that inherent drama into a meaningful benefit. . . . State your benefits in as believable a way as possible." It is fine to focus only on the positive side of things, but do not exaggerate or lie. You will fool no one. Design your marketing materials to attract people's attention. The most beautiful fliers do no good unless they are read. "Motivate your audience to get involved." You want them to do more than know about the product or service. You want them

# HOW ARE WE DOING?

Thank you for returning this form promptly. Your comments are vital to our being able to serve you, our customer, better.

Date: July 15, 2003

Name: John Doe                  Department: Sales

1. Was this information received by the time promised?   ☐ yes   ☐ no

   If "no," how was it? ☐ still in time ☐ too late, but useful anyway ☐ of no use

2. Was this information as expected?   ☐ yes   ☐ no
   If "no," why not? (check as many as apply)

   ☐ too much   ☐ too little   ☐ not specific enough
   ☐ off target   ☐ too old   ☐ other_____

3. Do you still need additional information on this subject?

   ☐ yes   ☐ no   If "yes," how can we help you? _____

   _____

4. Please estimate the value of this information to you. Include time saved or costs avoided.

   ☐ $0–$50   ☐ $50–$100   ☐ $100–$200   ☐ $200–$500   ☐ over $500

5. How courteous and helpful was the library staff in obtaining this information?

   ☐ very helpful   ☐ somewhat helpful   ☐ not very helpful
   ☐ very courteous   ☐ somewhat courteous   ☐ not courteous

6. If you checked anything other than "very," please tell us how we can improve.

   _____

7. Other suggestions or comments to make the library of more help to you?

   _____

**FIGURE 2-2   Customer Feedback Form (Sent to Customer)**

---

# HOW DID WE DO TODAY?

Thank you for returning this form promptly. Your comments are vital to our being able to serve you, our customer, better.

Name: _____    Department: _____

1. What was the purpose of this visit? Check all that apply:
   - ☐ to read a journal      ☐ to check out a book
   - ☐ to arrange a search    ☐ to order a document
   - ☐ to ask a question      ☐ to consult with a librarian
   - ☐ other _____

2. Did you find what you came in for today?    ☐ yes    ☐ no    ☐ not sure

   If you checked "no" or "not sure," what can we do to help? _____
   _____

3. Did you need to ask the library staff for help or instruction?    ☐ yes    ☐ no

   If "yes," did you experience a wait?    ☐ no wait    ☐ short wait
                                            ☐ long wait

   If "yes," how was the staff?

   - ☐ very knowledgeable    ☐ somewhat knowledgeable
          ☐ not very knowledgeable
   - ☐ very helpful       ☐ somewhat helpful       ☐ not very helpful
   - ☐ very courteous     ☐ somewhat courteous     ☐ not courteous

      If you checked anything other than "very," please tell us how we can improve. _____
      _____

   If "no," why not?    ☐ I already knew where to look
   - ☐ they were all busy    ☐ no time    ☐ I didn't think they could help
   - ☐ other _____

4. Other suggestions or comments to make the library of more help to you?
   _____

---

**FIGURE 2-3   Customer Feedback Form (Available in the Library)**

to take action—come in to the library, call on the phone, e-mail, or go to your website. "Be sure you are communicating clearly." Make a trial run to test the message to see if it is clear. "Measure your finished advertisement, commercial, letter, or brochure against your creative strategy." Even if it's the cleverest, cutest, or flashiest ad in the world, if it doesn't say what you want said, it's useless.

Trade your skills for those of others. For instance, offer a free search to a graphic artist in exchange for creating some graphics for your campaign, or offer a free library card to a printer who will run your fliers for free. If you have time, you can save a lot of money by doing your marketing in-house instead of hiring an expensive firm, but do this only if you have time, interest, and talent. Your campaign must look professional. Get ideas from nonlibrary marketing materials. Most professional associations (both library and those of your customers) have ideas and clip art that you can use. Take an ad you ran in the newspaper and reuse it for a flier or poster.

"Another way to promote a service, if funds are limited, is to get someone else to pay for it" (MacLeod and Ng n.d.). This is called cooperative marketing. For instance, your library can get free publicity by providing a prize for a contest or raffle at a conference or exhibition, the opening of a new store, a hospital health fair, or a company celebration. Books are the obvious choice, but you can also offer a certificate for a free search or document, a free library card, or a certificate for free photocopies. Vendors may pay for all or part of the advertising for their products and can even customize the advertising with your name or the name of your library. For instance, Dialog has provided covers for online searches, and the American Library Association can make posters or bookmarks with your picture and name for little more than for standard bookmarks. How about place mats for the cafeteria with your marketing logo and message on them? Or a crossword puzzle for customers to work while they eat with the message "Stuck for an answer? The library can help!"? Look for inspiration in the messages—at least the good ones—coming from pop culture (music videos, movies, television, music). Find an up-and-coming filmmaker and have him or her create a library infomercial. Distribute it through your local cable companies or organizational closed-circuit television network or even put it on your website as streaming video.

Here is one no-cost marketing idea that really worked. "To encourage company employees to stay current, [one librarian] challenged people to read one journal article every week." She posted abstracts of ten to fifteen articles per week for her customers to choose from (or they could find their own). "I know that customers are taking this challenge to heart, based on the document delivery requests that come in and on the in-house employees who have made it a weekly habit to spend a lunchtime in the library." She estimated that traffic in the library was up 25 percent in the first year of the program (Swart 2000).

## Marketing to Specific Types of Libraries

### LAW LIBRARIES

Several law librarians have told me that they now do very little *legal* research. The lawyers and paralegals can do most of it themselves using the major law information services. The librarians are now being asked to do research on medical, business, and international subjects, requiring a new set of skills for them. Once these skills are mastered, the library will have to market these services to the firm because it is a new type of library service. The marketing will have to be targeted and focused for specific practice groups; litigation has very different needs from those of the trust department.

A great marketing opportunity for law firm librarians is participation in client development (marketing). Find out who's in charge of client development and send him or her a letter or e-mail outlining specific ways in which you can help him or her to bring in new clients. You might even send some examples of materials you can supply. Then arrange a meeting with this person to discuss his or her actual needs at the moment. Once you know what he or she wants, provide it. Follow up to make sure the information was on target or to refocus if it was not. This will cost money, so make sure some of the budget for client development is allocated to the library. Arrange to be invited to meetings of the team and initial meetings with new clients so you can be sure you can obtain enough information about the client to target the information you provide.

Another value-added service that the law library can provide (and many already do) is coordination of continuing legal education (CLE) materials. (I suggest declining the job of keeping track of individual CLE progress, except for designing a database or Web page for the lawyers to track their own CLE.) Rosen (1999, 165) suggests that the library "require" CLE students to place course materials (books, tapes, etc.) in the library so they can be shared—or at least catalog them.

### ACADEMIC LIBRARIES

According to Robert H. Hu (2002), the faculty are the academic library's most constant customers. Students come and go, but faculty stay. They also have great influence over the library's operation, budget, personnel, collection policy, and so forth. Good relations with the faculty can make or break a library. Faculty also exert a great deal of influence over students and can fairly easily sway their opinions of the library. Marketing the competence of the library is extremely important.

Although a piece of information may have a useful life of only a day or two in a corporation, it may continue to be of use to a faculty member for years. Seldom will the academic librarian need to obtain a document in an hour. So marketing your speed of document delivery may not be as important as the wide range of libraries from which you can obtain materials. You will also want to market your expertise in teaching customers how to search resources (electronic and print) more efficiently and effectively. "There's much more emphasis in the university environment on giving the end user more skills to actually do a lot of the research themselves" (Richardson in Forbes 1998). Get professors to assign a library research project. Get referrals and testimonials from other departments you have worked with successfully. Show them how they'll benefit. Offer a "free" trial (Fosmire 2001).

Keeping in touch with your customers and their needs and habits is more difficult in the academic library. Not only do you deal with a large number of customers, but these customers (students and, sometimes, faculty) are constantly changing. The University of Michigan Business School library assigns a librarian as a liaison to the subareas of the school. At least once a year the liaison goes one-on-one with every faculty member to see about their needs (Soules 2001). If you do not have the staff to meet individually with all faculty, ask to be invited to regular faculty meetings. Be prepared to offer examples of how the library can assist faculty and students. Make sure that students are scheduled for a library tour and orientation very early in their academic careers, before they discover alternatives for themselves or form bad information-gathering habits (such as automatically going to the Internet first).

How can you reach customers when "everything" they need is online in their offices or dorm rooms? First, you need to get across the idea that "everything" is not on the Web. This can best be done with specific examples of incomplete information or misinformation you have found. Market the products and services that are *not* online (maps, reference books, handbooks, fiction, and the like). Finally, have exceptional customer service. One bad experience in the physical library and your customers will likely turn back to the Web to meet their information needs. My alma mater, Beloit College, is a small liberal arts institution in the Midwest that, in addition to being completely wired, has a wide-ranging offering of international educational experiences. The library director, Charlotte Slocum, supplied some of her ideas for marketing in a residential college where students can use library resources and services from their dorm or classroom, "from home on breaks, or while they're abroad or on an off-campus program." Turn everything into a marketing opportunity, even a chance meeting with a student or faculty member on the sidewalk. Develop a separate library Web page for off-campus library users containing resources and information they'll likely need. Develop Web-accessible library forms (like interlibrary loan forms) that users can use from wherever they are. Offer reference service via e-mail or phone. Provide proactive information to students at finals time about the many late-night places to study on campus (including the library). Host library coffee hours for faculty and staff. Slocum also developed an information literacy initiative targeted to faculty to build information literacy into their class assignments, worked with the admissions office on the script used by campus tour guides about the library so that it was more accurate and reflective of the wide range of services and resources, and encouraged the athletic department's idea to create library study tables for student athletes. Although students do not necessarily have to come into the library because the entire campus (dorms, study lounges, and classrooms) is wired, she notes, "Many students are attracted to working in the library by the open access to public computers. Our proactive reference staff use this as an opportunity to engage students about any information needs they may have and direct them to the most appropriate resources" (Slocum 2002).

Distance education is becoming more and more prevalent in the United States and has been the norm in many countries for years. Distance faculty and students need the library or its resources but don't have much contact with the library. The University of Nebraska–Lincoln established a website with access to databases and e-journals, a liaison librarian, and remote delivery of materials. Students can request items via e-mail or the Internet and can get materials the same way. The library sends a personalized welcome via e-mail, monitors student lists, and provides reference assistance (Adams 2002). Make sure that distance students and faculty know of all the services the library can provide and that customer service exceeds their expectations. Providing dial-in or Web-based feedback or reference service or both is also an opportunity for the library. Marketing can be accomplished electronically or by placing informative fliers in the materials sent out to the students.

## CORPORATE LIBRARIES

The for-profit world of business provides its own challenges to libraries. The higher placed the executive, the more likely he or she will not ask the library for help directly, instead sending a subordinate to locate information. This leads to misunderstandings, duplication of effort, and delays in providing the information. You need to convince management that it is in their own interest to communicate their information requests directly to the librarian. This will most likely take a face-to-face meeting with them. Bring along cost and time estimates of the time wasted by routing information requests through others.

## HOSPITAL LIBRARIES

Marketing to physicians is much like marketing to executives. Start at the top; send a letter to each department head asking to schedule a program on library services at a time and location of their choice. Make the presentation brief—no more than ten to fifteen minutes. Tailor it and the handouts for each department and be sure to follow up with individual physicians. Nurses face even stiffer time constraints and are often unable to visit the library. Schedule your presentations where they work, as did Kendall and Massarella (*see* the case study on page 41). "Serving each group of nurses in their own work areas, in their own time frames, proved that we were serious about supporting their information needs" (2001, 31).

Hospital libraries are getting involved more directly in patient care. This includes management of information and handouts to be given directly to patients (although this information still must be requested by and is often distributed by physicians or nurses). Some librarians even make rounds with the physicians or attend other physician meetings on a regular basis, providing quick literature searches on the spot or taking the questions back to the library and delivering answers later. Another point of patient contact is the consumer health library. Designed primarily for the community, sometimes it is also used by patients to learn more about their conditions or treatment.

## PUBLIC LIBRARIES

One form of marketing that you may not have thought of is referral. One department can refer clients to another department in the library, such as to a fee-based service, or the circulation staff can direct clients to the reference desk. Many libraries market to the youth market with extensive summer reading programs with tangible rewards for reading (certificates for food or movies are good examples of cooperative marketing); Internet access and, importantly, instruction; in-person or online help with homework (and homework-tracking programs for parents); and active promotion of the library as a "cool" place to study and meet peers.

What about going beyond this to create a special reading club just for teens during the school year? This would de-emphasize the library as a place and emphasize its informational or educational role.

There is one last piece of marketing advice I can share. "Above all, marketing is doing things. You can read all the books in the world, but if you don't put the advice into practice, nothing will happen" (Coote and Batchelor 1997, 1).

# 3 Publicity: The Tangibles

"Libraries have rarely focused their meager [publicity] efforts properly." (Scilken 1979, 11)

"Library [publicity] should be devoted to creating library supporters." (Scilken 1982, 2)

Publicity is "any information, promotional materials, etc. which brings a person, place, product or cause to the notice of the public. In the broadest sense, publicity is quite literally anything written or said, seen or heard about your business that communicates the who, what, why, when and where regarding your products/services or significant happenings" (Banker 2002, 1). My definition of publicity is everything that is on paper or in electronic form.

## CREATING AND WRITING A PUBLIC RELATIONS PLAN

To make the best use of your limited resources—time and money—you need to have a public relations (PR) plan. The plan doesn't have to be fancy or long, but it must exist and must be in writing. You might think it is difficult or time-consuming to write a marketing or publicity plan, but you can make it a very simple process. There's no need to start from scratch, either. Use a plan from another library or one of the many software programs available. You can also develop the plan yourself, or you can hire a consultant. If your parent organization has a PR or marketing professional on staff, use, or at least consult, him or her. If you don't have time or interest in writing the plan, a student or intern from a local library or business school would be thrilled to write it as part of an internship or practicum project. Finally, you don't need to plan everything at once, nor do you have to plan for a long period of time. "It is better to plan in depth the one or two most important [publicity] projects you can implement than to develop 15 projects that never get done" (Sirkin 1991, 4).

The process of planning is as important as, or even more important than, the final plan itself. The process forces you to look at where you are, where you want to be, and how you plan to get there. The plan should not be so detailed that you are locked into a plan that is no longer feasible. According to Coote and Batchelor (1997, 6), a good plan is short, "so that it will be read"; is adequately researched; contains achievable milestones and targets; is written, so everyone knows what he or she must do and so you can use it to get management support; and is both usable and used. You should expect to spend at least a week writing your plan.

The following outline introduces and explains the various parts of the PR plan.

I. Introduction

State why the plan is being written and its ultimate goal. Your goal may be to introduce a new service or product, to obtain additional funding (either from management or the community), to enhance the image of the library, or to raise awareness of the library within the community (such as with a summer reading program for youth).

II. Situational or Environmental Analysis

A. Market Summary

Describe the parent organization or community (the market), including geographic limits, demographics, description of segments, and how the target market receives information and finds out about new channels of information distribution. Include why the market is suitable for your library products and services, trends you expect for the future, and growth opportunities.

B. The Library Itself

Describe the library as it is now, its products and services, organizational culture, relationship with and status within the parent organization or community, information flows, any external mandates such as accreditation, what technology is installed (if applicable), staffing levels, and characteristics.

## C. SWOT Analysis

The SWOT (strengths, weaknesses, opportunities, and threats) Analysis is a very common technique for analyzing the environment in which the library operates or may operate in the future. It includes strengths (areas in which the library has strong capabilities or a competitive advantage or areas in which the library may develop capabilities and advantages in the time period covered by the plan); weaknesses (areas in which the library is lacking capabilities necessary to reach its goals or expected deficiencies); opportunities (situations outside of the library that, if capitalized on, could improve the library's ability to fulfill its mission, either now or in the immediate future); and threats (situations external to the library that could damage the library and should be avoided, minimized, or managed). Other useful evaluation techniques are Peer Comparison (benchmarking), Sector Analysis (often used to measure customer service), PEST (political, economic, societal, and technology) Factors, and Determinants of Service Quality (measures reliability, responsiveness, competence, access, courtesy, communication, credibility, security, understanding, and tangibles and can be very time-consuming).

## D. Current Customers

Who are your customers? What are their opinions of the library and its staff? Have these opinions changed recently? Why? Which of your services do they deem most valuable? Which could they do without? Who doesn't use the library? Why? What information do your users need? (Include both print and electronic information—and don't forget nonwritten information.) How does the informal network or grapevine work? Is the library in the loop? In which format or formats do your customers prefer to receive their information?

## E. Competition

Who are your competitors? Which of their products or services directly compete with yours? What are the sources of information for your nonusers? How did they manage before the library was established? Could they manage without the library? Who else in the organization or community is doing something others compare to (or confuse with) what you do? Include your analysis of who will be competitors in the future and what products and services they will be offering.

F. Current Services and Products

Describe specific features and benefits of your offerings, your competitive advantage, your current pricing strategy, and delivery options. If the plan is being written to market a specific product or service, give more detail on it, but include a brief description of other services so that the context can be seen.

G. Current Strategy

How do you make existing and potential customers aware of your products and services now? As above, provide more detail on the featured product or service if applicable. What has worked well for this product? What has not worked? Why are you trying to change strategy? What do you hope to accomplish?

III. The Plan

A. Vision and Mission Statements

A vision statement is what you would like the library to be at some point in the distant future. It should express your aspirations, core values, and philosophies. You should be able to state it in one short, memorable sentence. It should be idealistic, inspirational, exciting, and challenging. Your vision should be very general and not achievable—at least in the near term. The lifetime of a vision statement is at least five years and can be much longer. It should be stated in the present tense and be short. For example, the vision statement for the British Library is "The world's leading resource for scholarship, research and innovation."

A mission statement expresses what the library does, for whom it does it, how, and why. You can use more than one sentence, but the mission statement still should be relatively short (less than 100 words). It should contain measurable objectives and targets and should be achievable in the next three to five years. The library's vision and mission statements should closely parallel those of the parent organization. (Part of a library's mission might be to enhance the parent's reputation or, for a hospital library, law library, or research firm, to recruit staff.) In addition, a mission statement should reflect consensus and be unambiguous and understandable, accepted by the stakeholders, concise but complete, and memorable. If a library serves more than one clientele, the mission statement may reflect different services or levels of service to each group.

Here are some examples of good library mission statements. The Kresge Business Administration Library: "Connecting content and customers through access and service" (Soules 2001, 345). The Royal Society of Chemistry (a not-for-profit organization): "To operate in as business-like fashion as possible [and to maintain] high-quality after-sales service" (Hoey 1999, 47–48).

B. Objectives and Goals

Objectives are short, specific, measurable statements that fit and support the institution's mission. They must be achievable, flexible, motivating, and understandable. State what you intend to do, how you will know you've succeeded, and who is accountable.

Goals are objectives made real. They are often described as SMART: specific, measurable, achievable, realistic, and timely. Identify at least one specific outcome, for instance, "increase circulation by 10 percent in six months." Finally, set priorities. Priorities are goals ranked by order of importance.

C. Proposed Strategy

Strategies (or action plans) relate goals and priorities to daily activities. They are the final step in the planning process. Include the specific steps necessary to reach your goals, where you plan to position the library or service or product, what branding strategy you propose, and the specific publicity channels you will use.

IV. Resources Needed

A. People

Who is going to do the publicity? You? Someone on your staff? Are you going to hire an outside firm? Will have enough staff to meet the demand this campaign is designed to create? If not, how will you cope—add staff, cut other services? Will you need training for the staff? (Don't forget replacement or temporary staff if you will need to free permanent staff up for this project.)

B. Time

If you are not going to hire an outside firm, how will you or your staff find time to do the publicity? How will you have to rearrange schedules and responsibilities?

C. Equipment and Supplies

What physical materials will you need (paper, signs, computers)? Will you use what you already have, barter for it, or purchase materials outside? If you need a new computer for the campaign, what will you do with it when the campaign is over?

D. Budget

This is one of the hardest parts of the plan. Estimate the cost of everything: people, materials, services, and so on. Be able to justify every expense and double- or even triple-check your figures. I can't emphasize this enough: don't give the funders any unnecessary excuse to turn you down. Build in a "fudge factor" for unexpected expenses. If the campaign is to last more than a year, build in increases for inflation. Where is the money to come from? If you are in a corporate, medical, legal, or academic library, explain which departments will be approached for funding and whether you are going to try to recoup some of the funding from the customers by charging for your products or services. For a publicity plan to support a public library levy campaign, explain the benefits to the taxpayers and the overall community.

V. Implementation

A. Time Line and Milestones

When setting deadlines, allow time for unexpected problems. This will let you meet your deadlines without undue stress. Sometimes one step depends on the completion of another. To estimate the time to complete a project, make a list of all the parts of the project, decide how long each task will take, then add them up—and double the result. It is extremely important to monitor the progress of your plan, evaluating performance against the objectives. Put project milestones and those of all members of your staff on your calendar, or post a master calendar in a prominent location (on the wall of a conference room, for example) so that everyone can see how his or her particular responsibilities fit into the whole picture. All staff should be required to give periodic progress reports so you, as manager, can locate and avoid problems before they become critical. If someone gets behind, meet with him or her immediately.

B. Tactics

Tactics are short-term strategies and day-to-day activities. For example, "Place ad for new service in the daily newspaper, to run once a week for six weeks"; "Write article for the September in-house newsletter featuring one new service"; or "Arrange for campus library to be featured in orientation for all new law students."

C. Feedback Mechanisms

You must provide a way to monitor and measure the progress of your campaign. What is working and what isn't—and why? Are you reaching the target audience? What is their reaction? At regular intervals during the campaign, sample the target audience to see if they've seen or heard the message, if they've understood it, and if they have or will change their behavior because of it. The last is very important. Many customers see and understand publicity messages but do not purchase the product. You need to know why their behavior did not change. Perhaps you targeted the wrong people or promoted the wrong product. By getting feedback throughout the campaign, you can make changes along the way and improve your chances of success.

Feedback must be collected in a way that lets it be measured. To know that circulation was up is nice, but you need to know by how much (10 percent, 50 percent?). Your management will not be impressed by generalities.

VI. Supporting Documentation

Supporting documentation could include statistics or documents, a list of the members of the planning team, or a glossary of library or publicity terms.

## PUBLICITY BASICS

Most publicity falls into one of two categories. Direct promotion includes anything from a one-day open house in a small hospital library to the launch of a new branch of a public library. Other publicity is designed to create a favorable image of the library, to position or reposition it in the mind of the public, or to build on its reputation.

"Most [libraries] seem to run on the idea that the amount available for publicity is whatever can be saved on other activities, rather than putting in a specific sum" (Hamilton 1990, 7). To convince management of the need for spending time and money on publicity, show that it is (or should be) an integral part of providing professional library services, that it won't be overly expensive (assure them that you will spend the

## CASE STUDY

### FOLLOWING UP ON A SURVEY
**Women's College Hospital**
**Toronto, Ontario, Canada**

At the Women's College Hospital Library, in Toronto, use was static or declining (by one-third in one year), although efficiency was up. Accelerating budget cuts led to staff cuts, resource cuts, and user fees being implemented. At the same time, the staff experienced more demanding, sophisticated, and less loyal users. The staff did a survey to find out gaps in service and use patterns and to evaluate the current service. Most respondents were already regular users. Their responses provided follow-up actions for the library staff.

*Conclusions and Implications*

1. Even core users were using the library less because of lack of time.

   The staff decided there needed to be more training and more remote access.

2. Users wanted more information, more new services, more end-user access, and more training.

   The staff introduced fee-for-service Internet access and a training course with more publicity for both.

3. Electronic services were crucial.

   The staff made the online catalog available remotely via the Web.

4. Core users were willing to pay for new services.

   This led to a "virtual hospital" on the Web.

5. Users wanted more services at the desktop.

   The staff added order and delivery options on the Web.

6. There was interest in alternative providers.

   The staff added links to cooperating organizations on the Web page (Rashid and Burns 1998).

absolute minimum necessary to do a good job), that you can make the time to do it, that the effort won't detract from your supporting current library services and customers, and—this is very important—that you know what you're talking about (53). Should you hire a public relations professional or firm? On one hand, they produce a professional result (not that you couldn't do the same), save your time, and have any necessary special equipment. However, doing publicity yourself saves money, allows you to maintain control of the process, and avoids allowing an outsider access to in-house operations or business "secrets."

## Nine Publicity Tips

1. Be prepared. Know media deadlines, and have your publicity information ready so you can provide it to someone at a moment's notice.
2. "Find the real news hook—instead of fluff—in the stories you sell" (Seacord 1999, x). An increase in circulation statistics is not news, but a list of fifteen websites on a subject in the headlines makes a good story. (For instance, the activities of libraries and librarians right after the terrorist attack on the World Trade Towers on September 11, 2001, received a great deal of favorable press.)
3. Be professional. Follow established guidelines for the preparation of all press releases, public service announcements, photographs, and so on. Make sure your publicity is well written, cleanly typed, and free of spelling or grammatical errors. Photographs should be well composed and of good quality. When you go to meet a member of the press, dress and act professionally.
4. Take time to be organized. Have your materials in individual folders so that you can locate specific information quickly. Have all the facts at your fingertips when you make or receive a call from the press.
5. Check and recheck your copy. Make sure it answers the five *W*s and the one *H* (who, what, when, why, where, and how). Are all the contact details included? Obviously, all facts must be correct, quotes attributed, and permissions granted for testimonials and photographs.
6. Keep it simple. Don't put too much into any one publicity piece. It is better to send out two fliers, each with plenty of white space, than to send out one crowded piece. The extra cost can be justified because the money spent to send out unread publicity is money wasted.
7. "Remember that what your audience wants is information" (Seacord 1999, xi). Your publicity must be strategic, targeted,

comfortable, relevant, meaningful, interesting, and valuable. Tailor your publicity to the audience you want to reach.

8. Make your press releases and publicity stand out—but not too much. Use a distinctive letterhead and envelope, but make sure it still looks professional. We've all seen gimmicky mailings and ads that caught our attention but did not leave a favorable impression on us.

9. Finally, don't obsess over publicity. Yes, it is important, but it cannot be allowed to interfere with our main job—serving our customers.

Before you start writing, ask yourself: What is the purpose of the publicity piece? To promote underused or misunderstood services? To attempt to justify your existence? Who are you trying to reach? "Everyone" is not the right answer. New employees? New members of your community? People who have not used the library this year? Executives? Administrative staff? Researchers? Decision makers and funders? Different audiences should be targeted differently, so it is important to identify them clearly.

One way to ensure that the campaign is on target is to have other people review what you have written.

> Show it to others in the library and also a few people in your target market. Do they understand it? What questions do they have after reading it? Can they tell you what it means to them? When you show the piece to your intended audience, do not tell them what you want them to see. Instead ask them to read (or view) the piece and then ask them to explain what it said. Be sure to ask if they know what they are supposed to do after seeing the piece. For example, are they supposed to call the library, try a new product, or take some other action? If they do not know, then you need to ensure that your final product clearly states that. Finally, ask if the medium you have selected works for them. Will they view it? Will they be drawn to it? (Hurst 2001c, 9)

Harry Beckwith makes an important point about content: "Are you having trouble writing an ad for your [library]? Perhaps the problem is not your writing, it's your [library]—there's nothing special to write about" (1997, 13). If this is true, you should improve your library and its products and services *before* writing the piece—then you will have something to write about.

Although the appearance of your publicity is important, what is really important is the content—the message that you are sending. It's quite simple: "Identify the audience. Deliver the message. Supply a reason to 'get it.' Provide easy access for the purchase. If the message reaches the right people but concentrates on the features of the product, there is a high probability that it will be filtered out" (Seacord 1999, 3). Concentrate on the benefits. Don't waste your customers' time; get to the point. Make your publicity simple and quick to read. Mixed or overly complex messages confuse the customers. "Tell people—in a single compelling sentence—why they should buy from you instead of someone else" (Beckwith 1997, 199). Avoid negative advertising. Keep the message positive—what a product or service is or does, not what it isn't or doesn't. Avoid gimmicks. "If you think your promotional idea might seem silly or unprofessional, it [probably] is" (180). Don't overpromote or promise too much. Never send out generic publicity. Make it specific both to the sender (your library) and the recipient (the target). If you use clip art, personalize it. "You'll know you've succeeded in developing a simple but strong message when you hear someone generally believed to be outside the library circles repeating it" (Reed 2001, 5).

Advertising language should be conversational and relaxed, short, and simple. Avoid clichés like "committed to excellence," "proactive," "cost-effective." Make it dramatic, stimulate an emotion, make people curious, surprise people, and be different. "Psychologists at Yale University tell us that the most persuasive words in the English language are: you, money, save, results, love, health, easy, discovery, proven, new, safety, guarantee. To that list, I would hasten to add: free, yes, fast, why, how, secrets, sale, now, power, announcing, benefits, solution" (Levinson 1998, 144).

Two of the most powerful ways to get your message both noticed and remembered are a slogan and a mascot. A slogan should express something positive about the library and be short and easy to remember. Once you have chosen a slogan or mascot (or both), use them at every opportunity. They should appear on every piece of publicity: newsletters, posters, signage, ads, and handouts. If possible, they should appear on every piece of paper that leaves the library. One corporate librarian had a slogan "thrust" upon her. In a play on the online search engine, Ask Jeeves, a client started saying, "Don't ask Jeeves, ask Jenna!" Although she is not overly happy with the slogan, it is easy to remember, communicates the superiority of the librarian over the Web, and has stuck in the minds of her customers. In other words, it works. Another librarian had a similar experience. "I have to live with a slogan someone else invented as a first step for all our R&D projects: 'Say Grace.' Well, even if it is corny, it does help people remember my name and they should do a search before starting any new work" (McCarthy 1992, 291). The Iowa City Public Library created "Smart ALEC" (A Library Electronic

Connection) as the mascot for their online catalog. It is a "nerdy" drawing done by a local cartoonist and appropriate because Iowa City is the home of a major technical university. ALEC has been used in ads, signs, signage, T-shirts, a button, and newsletters. He was even used in advance of the launch of the software as a buildup and teaser. However, after two campaigns, he was put "on vacation" but may be resurrected at a future date (Eckholt 2001). This is a good example of not overusing one advertising campaign. Quit before the public gets tired of it.

Testimonials convey your message by association. If someone who is respected by the customer says that the library is wonderful, the customer will be inclined to believe it is true. Testimonials are most effective at or near the decision point, after the customer is already thinking about using your product or service. Use quotations from current or past customers, from authority figures (such as managers, doctors, lawyers, or politicians), or from experts (authors, professors, or respected journalists). Collect them from completed surveys, thank-you notes, or conversations or solicit them from your best customers (or, better, their managers). Don't push, but be specific when asking for a quote. Ask for an opinion of the product or service, how it helped them, how often they use it, why they use it, or a recommendation. Make sure you get written permission to use the testimonial, in the exact words you are going to use. If they don't give it, you can still use the quote but not attributed to them (say "a customer"). If you decide to use photographs with testimonials—a really good idea because "pictures speak louder than words" and people might recognize the face even if they don't recognize the name—use a professional photographer. Take the pictures right where the customer uses the product or service (such as in the lab or in their business). Be sure to get written permission from both the subject and the photographer. You can also use stories or anecdotes in your publicity. People really listen to stories and identify with them.

How your communications program looks is as important as it is for a product. Consistency across the entire spectrum of your materials is very important, especially in the use of color and graphics. Because sight is the critical sense, make sure all your publicity pieces look the same (or similar)—so they are recognizably yours.

## SPECIFIC FORMS OF PUBLICITY

### Brochures

If you're going to use a brochure, make it a good one. Emphasize the benefits the customer will get from using the library. Promote the features *they* consider important, not the ones you do. Consider creating a "family" of brochures with different messages for different services or for different audiences. This will not only focus the information in the brochure, but the brochure can be shorter. Make the brochure eye-catching and professional. Use photographs and graphics, but not the same tired old ones—the open book or the computer terminal; use something different and directly related to the message you are sending. Design the front panel to catch the reader's attention and invite him or her to read more. Proofread all materials well—typos and errors are especially embarrassing for librarians. It is *very* important to make sure the full name of the library and its address, phone, fax, e-mail, and website are in an easy-to-see location. Write in short, clear sentences. Try a question-and-answer format. You can create a three-panel brochure out of 8½-by-11-inch paper. (Microsoft has trifold brochure templates that will help you to place information in the right place so the brochure looks right when folded. *See* <http://search.officeupdate. Microsoft.com/TemplateGallery/ct88.asp>.) One last but extremely important point. Publicity materials do no good in a drawer or even on a table in the library. Hand them out to everyone, everywhere. Put them in the cafeteria or break room. Carry one or two with you everywhere you go.

## Business Cards

When you meet someone, you need to make a "powerful, positive, personal impression" and present a sophisticated, professional image (Hiam 2000, 224). To make your card (and you) stand out and be remembered, try a quotation, a different layout, a special logo, or even a better grade of card stock. But don't be too different. A vertical layout is distinctive but is harder to read in most business card files. Your cards should match your letterhead.

If your parent organization has a standard business card format, you will have to use it, of course, but you may be able to create your own for some uses (such as at professional conferences). If your parent organization does not provide business cards, you definitely should make your own. You can purchase them at nearly every office supply store or printer, or you can make them on your own computer or even order them over the Web. Include your degrees on your card (if policy allows) to remind people that you are a professional. (Judith A. Siess, B.A., M.A., M.S. looks much more impressive than just Judith A. Siess.)

## Newsletters

Every library should have a newsletter. They are relatively easy and inexpensive, allow you to express your personality and values, are a very flexible format, and are good relationship builders. Your newsletter can show current or potential customers what's new or important in the library or their areas of interest, advertise products or services, build the library's image, and remind customers that you are there to assist them. What should you include in a newsletter? New services, additional information about underutilized services, recent acquisitions (books, journals, even standards or pictures), professional activities of the librarian, excerpts from articles by you in professional journals, or testimonials from satisfied customers. A good column idea is to feature sample questions answered recently. "They always generate additional inquiries, which proves that people read the newsletter. We also hear comments like 'I didn't know the library could provide that kind of information,' which tells us that, as much promotion as we do, we apparently still need to do more" (Edwards in La Rosa 1992, 58).

Keep your newsletter simple and easy to read, remembering all the hints listed under brochures. The format of the newsletter must be consistent, not only with your other publicity materials, but from issue to issue. There should be a masthead at the beginning that should contain the name of the newsletter, the library's name, the date, volume, and number. If you have a slogan or mascot, you may want to use it in the masthead, although you can also put the slogan at the end of the newsletter and sprinkle smaller graphics (of the mascot or other images) throughout the issue. Mix long and short articles. Funny stories, jokes, puzzles, or cartoons (remember to observe copyright rules) are a good addition but should make up a relatively small part of the whole. Headlines should relate to the story, be specific, and be in the present tense. If there is a lot of text, columns make for easier reading, as does liberal use of white space.

Your newsletter should appear on a regular, predictable basis, ideally monthly but at least quarterly. Don't start a newsletter unless you or the library can commit to continue it and you can meet the added service demands that the publicity may produce.

An e-mail newsletter is "just-in-time" publicity that is interactive, current, inexpensive, cheap, and easy. It can be offered by subscription, by using an electronic list, or by posting the newsletter on your website. You may want to consider having multiple newsletters, each aimed at a different target market. What is interesting or important to one group may be boring to another and give them a good excuse to stop reading. Include no more than five or six short articles and a couple of regular features—no more than four pages when printed out. Start articles with the conclusion or benefit to the reader. Make headlines clear and able to stand alone. Cover only one subject per paragraph, and use bullets freely. Promote your e-newsletter by word of mouth, in print, or by e-mail—the most effective way. It should come out no more often than weekly.

## Press Releases

> It's not newsworthy until journalists know about it. (Hiam 2000, 161)

The press release lets journalists know of the wonderful things your library is doing. It is very important to follow the proper and accepted format for notifying the press. A press release should have five sections:

1. The headline. This is the "hook," designed to catch the reader's attention. Some writers say not to try to write a catchy headline—let the reporter or editor do this. Instead, type a subject in caps, centered at the top.
2. The byline. This is simply the city and state from which the release is issued and the date of the release (or "For Immediate Release").
3. The lead (first) paragraph. It should cover the five Ws and one H (who, what, when, why, where, and how—in that order) and should be no more than 40 to 100 words.
4. The rest of the text and images. Do not repeat the information in the lead paragraph. Provide background and context for the story. Make it interesting, not a boring list of names and dates. Include quotations and photographs. Use "the library" or names instead of "we," "our," and "you." Don't use superlatives; they will be edited out. Write simply, in short paragraphs. Put "-more-" at the end of each page and "-30-" or "###" at the end of the release. If you send photographs (a good idea), they should be 8-by-10-inch glossies with the caption on a separate piece of paper. Be sure that you get permission (a release) from all the people photographed, especially your clients. State that you have the releases in the caption of the photo. Press releases should be one page in length; go to two pages only if it is unavoidable. The entire release should be fewer than 250 words.
5. Contact information. Be sure to include the name of the organization or library, your name, the address, phone and fax numbers, e-mail address, and (if desired) your website URL.

A press release must have a short, clear, unique cover letter "that tells the reporter why you think he or she should write about your company" (Hiam 2000, 171). Target your release. Make sure the publication will be interested in what you have to say. (Don't send a release about a new children's story hour to *Modern Maturity*, for example.) Small community newspapers are always looking for local stories and reach many people.

Don't address the letter or release to "Editor"; get the name of the editor or reporter—and spell it right. Know the paper's deadlines, and provide your information to them at least ten days in advance of the event or the date you want the story to appear. Note: many reporters are unaware that there are libraries (and especially professional librarians) such as corporate, medical, law, or other nonpublic libraries. Often they are surprised and very interested in writing a story about them. Talk to reporters and editors at times other than when you need them. If your story isn't printed, don't bother the editor. You may check (once) briefly to make sure it was received. Don't sweat rejection. "In fact, you are more likely to be covered by a journalist who has rejected you in the past than by one who has never heard of you" (Hiam 2000, 171). Follow up on press releases. Find an excuse to call the reporter (a new development, for instance). Definitely keep track of what you sent to whom and when. When you are mentioned in the press, make the most of it. Use the clipping on your website or on posters, and send it to your customers and, very importantly, your boss.

Go to <http://www.BusinessWire.com> or <http://www.PRNews wire.com> to see press releases from various organizations. A press release template for Microsoft Word is available at <http://search.office update.Microsoft.com/TemplateGallery/ct93.asp>.

You may also want to create a media kit. This is usually a folder with two inside pockets containing one or more news releases, photographs, a fact sheet with background information, and a contact name (which can be your business card). Put a catchy but classy sticker on the front with the name of your library. You can find details on creating press kits in Stephanie Seacord's *Public Relations Marketing: Making a Splash without Much Cash.*

## Direct Mail

Direct mail refers to all advertising materials that are sent directly to the individual customer, as opposed to posters, billboards, and commercials, which are "broadcast" to a wide audience. Direct mail is usually targeted to a selected group of theoretically interested people. There are several misperceptions and myths about direct mail. Let's look at them.

*Myth 1:* "Direct mail is junk mail." Believe it or not, the majority of direct mail is at least opened and scanned. With direct mail you have control—over the medium and the message, the form, and who receives the message. "You rarely compete side by side with rival advertising messages. Your ad is not going to fight an ad on the opposite page. Your message is not sandwiched between two other commercials" (Bacon 1992, 6). A small library, with the help of quality printing and personalization, can look as good as a large one.

A direct mail letter should include a description of the product or service you are "selling," its features and benefits to the customer, any costs involved, and, most importantly, a request for action. Be sure to tell the customer how he or she can respond ("Stop in and ask us a question," "Bring in this coupon for a free library tour [or search]," "Call us for more information," or whatever you want him or her to do next). Make the reply easy, preferably free, and give the customer several reply options (e.g., phone, e-mail, fax, online). You do not need to limit your letter to one page; in fact, a three-page letter does better at establishing trust than a one-page letter. Personalize the letter with the person's name—you will get twice the response. Writing the address in large letters (especially the name) will increase the appeal to the reader. You can bring a partnership feel to non-face-to-face transactions by inserting names, handwritten notes, comments, or suggestions for further service ideas on invoices and other communications (like amazon.com's suggestions for books readers might enjoy).

Write in a casual tone. Use lots of white space, and try printing the most important sentences in color. Other good techniques are a "teaser" on the envelope, such as "Free offer inside," or ending the letter with a "P.S." (maybe even handwritten) that reinforces the message. Coupons and reply forms are good publicity vehicles. Put an address sticker on the back so it is easy for recipients to tell you sent it. In addition, if you code the address by adding a box or room number specific to each mailing, you'll know to which piece of publicity they are responding. If you need a reply, preaddress the form with the library's address, and you will increase the response. Of course, if you send a prestamped reply envelope, you will really increase the response rate, but you will also increase your cost. Where is the best place for direct mail ideas and suggestions? Your mailbox. Adopt those techniques that attract your attention (Bacon 1992, 11). Finally, be sure to follow up on your mailings with a quick phone call to make sure the mailing arrived and to answer any questions. A letter can only do so much.

When it comes to addressing your mailer, "the most important element is the right list" (Levinson 1998, 213). Choose your target audience carefully. A list is either right or it isn't. You can have the greatest offer, nicest-looking letter or brochure, or the most important message, but if you are aiming at the wrong people, you will not get the results you are seeking. The mailing list determines 50 to 60 percent of direct mail's effectiveness. The creative message, or package, only counts for 5 to 20 percent (Tolman 1998, 36). Creating your own marketing database is time-consuming and therefore expensive but is more likely to produce the results you want than a bought list. Keep it current. It is estimated that 10 percent of addresses go bad each year.

*Myth 2:* "There is no such thing as an average [direct mail] response rate; there can't be. The sole benchmark of your success should be your profits [or statistics]" (Bacon 1992, xiii). If you think the response rate for direct mail seems low, compare response rate per dollar spent to other kinds of publicity (television, radio, newspapers, etc.). Because direct mail is less expensive, it can support a lower response rate.

Sometimes it is better to outsource direct mailing. Hire outside help when you don't have time to do a great job of it, when you've gotten poor response from your mailings, or when you just don't have the creative knack. "Some direct mail gets opened by 90 percent of its recipients" (Bacon 1992, xi). First-class letters are opened more often than bulk mail. If you must use bulk mail, use a meter or, better, a stamp.

If you can, send mail to your list often, maybe even as often as every six weeks. They may already be customers, but you have to remind them or they'll respond to your competitors' pitches.

## Reports and E-mail

The annual report is an especially good publicity tool. Distribute it widely or, if it is very long, just the executive summary. Place copies at the circulation or reference desk. Because you use good graphics, style, and good writing to make it interesting to your managers, it will be easy for your customers to read as well.

Writing in a positive, professional style is especially important with e-mail. You never know to whom the recipient will forward the e-mail; a hastily written or nasty note is very likely to come back to haunt you.

## Bulletin Boards and Display Cases

A bulletin board is a great way to publicize your products and services easily and for almost no money. If a permanent bulletin board is not feasible, consider using a portable easel that you can move around. Use the display case as a superboard. Take advantage of its depth to create three-dimensional displays. Make sure the bulletin board or display case is placed in a high-traffic area. This may or may not be near the library itself. Near the cafeteria is always a good location. Other good places are near coffee or snack machines, near the main entrance or exit of the building, or even close to the rest rooms. You could also mount an exhibit in windows of vacant stores in the area. You can extend the physical presence of your library by creating displays in other locations.

It is important to make the bulletin board easy and simple, something people can relate to. The use of stories, puns, and humor is especially appropriate. Unlike the billboard, you should try to make sure the viewer (customer) has to take time to read the bulletin board, not just glance at it as he or she passes by. You do this by using "clutter" (lots of material on the board) or lists. Enlarge a page from one of those Word-a-Day calendars (such as "Merriam Webster's 365 New Words Calendar" from Workman Publishing). This is both interesting and educational. Cartoons about libraries or computers are always good. Dilbert is a real crowd pleaser for a corporate library. Be sure you follow copyright laws: don't make a copy; use the original. (I bought a Dilbert daily calendar and posted the cartoon each day. Some people came in every day to check out Dilbert and maybe checked out a book or two.) Feature library users, complete with their photographs and quotes from them about how the library has helped them. If you can get management to participate, that's even better. You might also want to feature one of the library staff or volunteers. If your organization is into statistics, post graphs of performance measurements, using color if possible. Purchase posters from most library associations or suppliers, or, better, pick them up for free at conferences. The American Library Association (ALA) "Read" posters are very eye-catching, and there is one for almost every taste. Post pictures of your latest library open house or other event. People *love* to see their own faces.

If you do a daily or weekly summary of news stories, post that on the bulletin board so that those who are not on the list will still be able to keep up. Display copies of articles or books written by or about your customers. Lists of new books are nice if they are accompanied by strong graphics; otherwise, they can be boring. Publishers go to a lot of trouble to make book jackets attractive—use this expertise to make your bulletin board interesting.

Be sure to change the display frequently. People will lose interest if you do not change it regularly. In a library for a small biotechnology firm, I placed a new chemical formula pun on the bulletin board every week, with the answer the following week. (Example: $NaCl$ + DieHard = assault and battery.) It got people to look at the bulletin board regularly. Build a display around an event or a holiday. Check *Chase's Book of Events* or various websites for ideas.

Donna McLaughlin-Shuereb, a columnist for *Church and Synagogue Libraries* and a volunteer at the Wyandotte Catholic Consolidated Schools Library and First United Methodist Church in Wyandotte, Michigan, suggests picking a concept (such as a fruit stand, camera, clothing) and thinking of all the words that can be associated with it. Then relate each word to the library (1998). For example, if you choose zoo animals as your subject, use these phrases: You otter [ought to] read a book. I'd be lion [lying] if I didn't tell you that our books are great. You might also use anything directly relating to your organization (operating room, cubicle, courtroom, etc.) or group jokes and puns around a theme. Use pictures from magazines or advertisements if you wish. Get in the habit of clipping good pictures whenever you encounter them and putting them in a "bulletin board" folder.

## Giveaways, Takeaways, and Other Ideas

People love to pick up things to take home. Giveaways can be inexpensive publicity for your library, but make sure that everything sends the right message. Use your established color scheme and mascot or slogan. Make sure the library's name, address, phone and fax numbers, e-mail address, and URL appear on *all* takeaways. Magnets are always popular and are quite inexpensive in bulk. Use one of the nonrectangular shapes that are now available (they do not cost more). You can put just your contact details on them, or you can use them to promote a specific product or service. Sticky notes are well received, but once they are gone, your message is lost. How about putting them in a plastic carrying case with your message on the front? These cases can be refilled so that your message will stay in front of the customer. Most people like buttons, but they can be expensive. If you will be using buttons often, consider buying a button-making kit. It will cut your costs considerably. T-shirts are rather expensive but can be used as prizes in reading contests, as gifts for volunteers or campaign contributors, or even for staff to wear on special occasions. You can also sell them to raise money. The ALA has many bookmarks from which to choose, but my favorite is one with the librarian's picture and information customized for your library. For National Library Week, one law library distributed laminated place mats—with proofreading symbols on one side and the firms cite-checking style guide on the other—to associates and paralegals "who often ate lunch at their desks because they were so busy cite-checking and proofing briefs" (Curci-Gonzalez 2000, 16). You could easily adapt this idea to your own library. Another librarian distributed a quiz about the library from a display table in the cafeteria. She also distributed fliers with the answers in them. All correct quizzes were entered in a drawing for a book. I'm sure you can think of many other ways to use this often-overlooked location as a place to publicize the library.

Create a cover for search results or document delivery that promotes the library or other products and services. Use your slogan or mascot. You also may be able to get these covers free from one of the search services. Bumper stickers are good for image creation or for a specific purpose, such as a levy campaign. They extend the reach of your publicity to the community at large. Obviously, they are more appropriate for a public library or for a not-for-profit charitable institution.

Often forgotten is the power of the written word. Consider writing a letter to the editor. "One way we can make a contribution to library advancement is to write a letter a week to the media about some aspect of library service. *We* have to tell local people what libraries are about, what librarians should be doing and do it well" (Scilken in Deitch 2002, 56). There are e-mails, postcards, and personal letters. Write for publication, but remember that magazine articles or ads should involve the reader and suit the tone of the magazine. Choose quality publications—their quality will rub off on your message.

Television and radio can be used for news items, public service announcements (PSAs), and interviews. Because television is a visual medium, it is good for demonstrations. (Don't forget about cable stations.) Other good ideas for publicity are a "wall of fame" with testimonial letters from satisfied customers, a "prescription" pad for physicians with a referral to the library for more information, or a list of the top ten websites in your customers' subject area.

## THE COMPUTER AS SALESPERSON: USING TECHNOLOGY

The computer has changed the way we market our products and services. Our customers make fewer visits to the library, resulting in less opportunity for in-house publicity, bibliographic instruction, and relationship building, so we have to find ways to market to them electronically. The primary means of electronic marketing are e-mail and the library website, but you can also use newsgroups, chat rooms, message boards, and electronic discussion groups to inform your customers about the library. We need to position ourselves in the mind of our customers as *the* experts in navigating and making the best use of the Internet. It is in our best interest to take advantage of this two-way medium to communicate product and service information to our customers; to facilitate our customers' complaints, preferences, and ideas for improvements; and to improve our products and services based on these suggestions.

## E-mail

Nearly everyone has access to e-mail these days. If your organization allows you to offer Internet or e-mail access, promote it. Employees who come in to check their e-mail may come back to use other library resources later. If you can, put a banner ad on the library terminals to advertise your products and services, emphasizing the electronic. Although many electronic discussion lists prohibit advertising, most will not object to a short message in your signature file as long as it is short, simple, and discreet. For instance, my signature file reads as follows:

> Judith A. Siess
>
> Information Bridges International, Inc. /I\B/I\
>
> Author of *The Visible Librarian: Asserting Your Value with Marketing and Advocacy*, American Library Association (0-8389-0848-9)
>
> Publisher of *The One-Person Library: A Newsletter for Librarians and Management*
>
> [My contact information] . . .

You'd be surprised how many inquiries I get from people who see this short advertisement at the bottom of all my e-mail messages.

## Web Pages

"The information used by an organization as it conducts its business can no longer be physically restricted to the library or information unit as advances in electronic delivery methods have allowed the delivery of information directly to employees' desktops" (Henczel 2001, xxi). Customers at branch offices, medical clinics, partner hospitals, dormitories and classrooms, branch libraries, and home are now able to access the library and its services nearly as well as those who walk in our doors.

The primary selling point of a website is its content. We librarians are the experts at content acquisition, classification, and access. It is highly unlikely that the information technology (IT) department (the computer people) will consider content and classification their highest priorities. Librarians must be involved to keep the focus on these two concepts, which are ultimately more responsible for the success of a website than programming and graphics. Working with the IT group raises that group's awareness of the library. Librarians can and should be involved as planners, marketers, leaders (visioneers), risk takers, and partners with customers and vendors.

Another wonderful opportunity the Internet offers is the ability to create online communities of library users. The librarian is the optimal person to set up internal electronic discussion groups or bulletin boards to facilitate communication within the organization or with outsiders. I have long thought that such communication could avoid many meetings. Why not post the issues to be considered and have the discussion take place asynchronously (not all at the same time) online? No wasted time trying to get everyone together, no travel time, no verbal arguments. If policy allows, you could even take votes online. This should be the future of meetings in the twenty-first century—and librarians can lead the way.

Enough of generalities. Let's get down to the nitty-gritty of making your website a better publicity vehicle for your library. First, decide on the purpose of the site. Is it to promote the library to internal customers, people in their homes, or customers outside the organization? Is it to be a gateway to your own electronic information or your collection or will it just provide descriptions of library services? Next, determine what you want to include. Keep it short and simple. Fancy graphics and frames may look really cool, but they will add to the load time and may not work well on all computers. This is especially true if customers are at home or if they will be dialing up from laptops or other systems with limited modem speeds and bandwidth. Most customers and we librarians want information, not flash. If you use frames, it is best to provide a non-frames option on the front page. If you provide an alternative-language version of the site, make it easy to select the proper language—on the home page, in Spanish or French or Vietnamese or whatever.

The basics elements of a library website should be

a brief description of your community or parent organization;

a brief description of your library with complete contact details (address, telephone and fax numbers, e-mail address, and URL);

the names, credentials, and subject specialties of the library staff—both professionals and nonprofessionals. If possible, include photographs;

the library's hours and location (if it's hard to find within the building, campus, or community, add a map);

major library services, including any special collections. Feature new items or services prominently on the first page;

a short version of your circulation or use policy. "All citizens of XYZ county upon furnishing proof of residency" is better than "anyone in XYZ county." Likewise, "all physicians with admitting privileges, nurses, technicians, support staff, patients, and members of the community if they have a referral from a physician" is clearer than "employees of the hospital and the public";

a page listing your products and services, specifying those for which there is a charge;

information on access requirements. If your site requires the use of any special software or add-in, or if it will merely work better with it, be sure to note this prominently on the front page. If the software or add-in is available for free on the Web, provide a link to it. The same goes for a password. If customers need one, tell them how to get one, preferably via e-mail; and

general information and a way to get back to it. Every page should include the date each page was last updated, your organization's name and the name of the library, the name and e-mail address of the Webmaster, and a "back" button.

Because your users will be interested in other sites, put links to them on your site. Get customers in the habit of going to the library page to start their Web searches because you have the links they need. Make it easy for customers to submit new sites, suggestions, questions, and requests. Use a reply form, but also include an e-mail address and telephone and fax numbers. You can also create personalized library portals for your customers with a customized list of resources, suggestions for books or articles based on past search patterns and journal use, a list of items checked out or ready for pickup, or even online renewal or hold options. You might also want to put photos of the library or library events on the Web page so that far-flung users can feel connected.

As Bonnie Shucha points out, "Aesthetics are also important" (2002, 12). If the site style is outdated, users may assume the content is outdated as well. You want the pages to look good, but—more importantly—you want them to be easy to use and to work well. Think like your customers. How might they look for information? Put the information they are most likely to want most on the front page with click buttons to important areas of the site. Leave some white space for readability. Be consistent. Similar information (like the "back" or "next" buttons) should look similar and should appear on the same place on each page. As you surf the Internet, note any site that you encounter that looks bad or doesn't work well and avoid the same mistakes.

If possible, mount your site at a temporary address and have some of your customers (including those off-site) test it. Ask them to be very critical, and incorporate their suggestions if at all possible. Test your site using several different browsers to make sure it works well with all the browsers potential customers might use (not everyone uses Explorer or Netscape). Proofread your pages very carefully; then have someone else proof the pages, too. It is not good for your image to have spelling or grammar errors on your Web pages.

Finally, plan a campaign to make your users aware of the website. Send out e-mails and memos. Place an article or interview in the in-house magazine. Announce it at company or department meetings. Schedule a demo or open house where customers can try out your site with you there to answer questions. Put your website address on everything going out of the library. Establish reciprocal links with similar organizations and even departments within your organization. (Reciprocal means you link to their site and they link to yours.) Depending on your organization's policy, you may want to publicize your new website on the World Wide Web itself. You can send press releases to electronic newsgroups, lists, and print journals that your target audiences read and distribute fliers within your organization or community.

Make sure search engines and users can find you. Choose Web page titles carefully, both for content (for search engines) and for length (for bookmarks). Use only lowercase for the titles; this makes it easier for customers to remember and type in the URLs. Use only alphanumeric characters with no spaces; leave out articles (a, an, the), but include the library's name. Make sure your file names are descriptive, for example, librarycatalog.html, not cat.html. Add metatags to the document header with keywords that surfers might use to find your site. In the description, which is displayed by some search engines, include a couple of sentences describing the site content well, with the library's name. Repeating words in metatags does not increase your site ranking in most search engines. Use services such as Submit It! <http://www.submit-it.com>, Register-It! <http://www.register-it.com>, and Internet Promotions <http://www.websitepromote.com> to inform the most popular search engines of your site. Periodically search for your own site. If it is not coming up under the appropriate keywords, modify your metatags. Finally, make your home page the default for all computers in the library.

You say you don't have time to do all this? If you want a good Web presence, you will have to find time. If the cost of the website is to come out of your budget, make sure you will have additional funds to cover it. You may also outsource the design and maintenance of the website. If you do, allow plenty of lead time, both for the bidding and design processes. It is a lot of work developing and maintaining a website, but it is increasingly expected of the library. Done well, it shows that you are a master of the new technology, user-oriented, and up-to-date. It also is a new challenge to keep you fresh and excited and provides excellent exposure for you and the library in this increasingly Web-centered age. Don't be afraid of it—enjoy it.

# 4 Public Relations: The Personal Touch

"We need to remember that the information profession is a people business. We provide a service *for* our clients, not *to* them." (Infield 2002, 12)

## PUBLIC RELATIONS BY WALKING AROUND: GET OUT OF THE LIBRARY

You can only do so much with publicity. Sooner or later you will have to meet your customers face-to-face. Because you cannot count on your customers actually coming into the library, you will have to leave the library and go to them. There are many advantages of going to the user—in his or her workplace. You break down the real or perceived physical barriers between you and the customer. You can talk to the customer directly, not through an intermediary such as a secretary, law clerk, intern, or colleague. Because most people are more comfortable in their own space, you may be able to talk to the customer at greater length, giving you more chance to explore other information needs and opportunities besides the current problem. In some cases, you may even meet a customer face-to-face for the first time, after having communicated via e-mail or telephone. By taking the time and trouble to go to the customer, you are demonstrating that his or her needs are important to you—more important than whatever you were doing in the library itself.

Whenever possible, deliver items to customers in person. This gives you the chance to ask the customer, "Is this what you wanted? Is there anything else I can do for you?" If things are quiet in the library or you just need a physical or mental break, go for a walk around the facility. Often, after talking with someone new, I run across an article or news item that would interest this person, which I send to him or her with a note and an invitation to stop into the library. Voilà! A new customer. In addition, just being seen around the organization is a form of public relations (PR), reminding current and potential customers that there is a librarian available to help them. People who would never take the time to come into the library, send an e-mail, or even pick up the telephone to call you may stop you in the hall with a question. Always carry a pen or pencil and some paper (or sticky notes or index cards) with you to remind you who asked which question.

Visit a department or area of the community you know little about or in which you have few customers. Ask questions, get people's names, distribute brochures and business cards, and offer your services. Keep it casual. Follow up with a thank-you note or memo. Have a one-on-one talk with the head of a different department or a different area of your constituency each month. Attend open houses and in-service education programs for other departments. Serve on committees, even inviting them to meet in the library if there's room.

In one corporation, I found that most branch office personnel thought that the library was just for headquarters staff. I arranged visits to the major branch locations. I started with a short presentation on the library's products and services, then took a tour of the facility. I distributed brochures and business cards to every department and set up times for individual consultations. When I returned home, I found that inquiries from the branches increased markedly.

Public libraries and not-for-profit organizations can reach a lot of customers and increase community awareness by making speeches or having a booth at neighborhood festivals, county fairs, or block parties. Hospitals with consumer health libraries and law firms that do pro bono work or reference for a fee could do the same. Community-service organizations like Kiwanis, Rotary, or Lions are always looking for a free speaker, and these businesspeople are potential customers and "influence leaders" in the community. Take the opportunity to influence potential librarians by speaking at school career days. Even corporate libraries can participate; few people even know that there are libraries in corporations. When you go out to talk to people, be on time and do your homework; know something about the audience (even if it is an audience of one). Use a person's name frequently—and pronounce it properly. Listen actively and intently; make eye contact. "The trick is to not start the conversation out of nowhere, but to come in with the right facts at the right time—then mention that the information center has lots more where that came from" (Dempsey 2002, 78).

You say you don't have time to "walk around" or to serve any more customers. "If you truly have so many patrons and so much work that you don't want to draw any more patrons to the library, I understand. I also realize that finding time to socialize is easier said than done. However, a few minutes socializing can only help our image and our libraries. Being a friendly, outgoing librarian is not a bad thing. Try it" (McClellan 2001, 8-9).

## TEACHING AS PUBLIC RELATIONS

> "Libraries are institutions designed for use. To be used, libraries must be familiar to user groups." (Buchanan in Karp 1995, ix)

Library systems and services may be unfamiliar to our customers, and their instructions all too often are written in what seems to our users to be a foreign language. Not wanting to appear ignorant or stupid, especially in front of their colleagues, they may be reluctant to ask questions. Training on library systems and services is not part of their job description and therefore is not a high priority. But there are ways to make library training essential for students of all kinds—from corporation heads to students—and serve as PR for your library at the same time.

### Presentation Skills

Put yourself at ease by being organized and well prepared. The old formula of "tell them what you're going to tell them, tell them, and tell them what you told them" still works, but you may want to call the first part "learning objectives" or "goals." Arrange your presentation in a logical progression. End with a summary of your main points and something humorous, memorable, or that the audience can put into immediate use.

"The single most important thing you can do to be more comfortable with public speaking is to practice" (McMillen 2001). Rehearse your entire presentation, out loud. You do not speak the way you write, so you need to find words, phrases, and timing that fit your personal style and allow you to feel comfortable. If you tend to speak quietly, practice speaking loudly without shouting. Join a local Toastmasters or other speakers club, a community theater group, or take a class in speech or communications at a local college or adult education program to gain practical speaking experience.

### Adult Education Skills

For many of us, education brings to mind high school or college. Adult education is different. Students are not required to attend and therefore require a high-quality presentation that will both keep their interest and be of practical value. It should be a dialogue, not a speech. Just as different people teach differently, different people learn differently. Use a variety of audience participation activities, including break-out groups, role-playing, and written or oral exercises. Ask questions and listen to the answers. Call on the shy students and control the talkative ones. At the end of each section, pause to make sure that the message has been understood. Don't wait until the end of the presentation or the evaluation form to find out that you lost your audience about fifteen minutes into the class.

## Content Skills

All the presentation skills in the world will not make up for not knowing your subject cold. Combine theory and practice to create an interesting presentation that participants can implement when they get back to their offices or homes. Use anecdotes or stories to illustrate your points and bring the real world into the classroom. Ask the students for examples from their own experience. Don't try to cover too much in one session. It is better to give a sample of the services and products you can provide than to list them all. Provide students with additional information in the form of handouts.

## Tools

There are many fancy tools that you can use in your teaching: PowerPoint, overheads, and slides, for instance—but I don't use them. Overheads take your eyes off the audience and are distracting. Slide projectors can jam. Computers can go down. A PowerPoint presentation could just as well have been sent via e-mail. Internet connections are often lost in the middle of a presentation. Low tech has its advantages; handouts are always there. At the beginning of a workshop I hand out an outline of my presentation, with a bit of space for notes. At the end, I provide another with my lecture notes, additional resources, and readings for students. A minimum of structure and technology leaves you free to improvise. If the group seems to grasp a concept quickly, you can skip to the next topic, or you can spend more time in an area of special interest. Not dimming the lights keeps the attention where it belongs, on you and the students, not on the slides or overheads. Be sure you have a blackboard, whiteboard, or flip chart so you can write down important points, topics for further discussion, or additional information.

Teaching about electronic resources poses additional problems. Emphasize that you are not expert in every aspect of every resource, but that you will find out the answers to any problems that arise. Make sure that you don't teach more than they want to learn. Give students an overall idea of the possibilities of the resource; save the details for one-on-one sessions later, or cover them in detailed instructions you hand out after the presentation. Include a live demonstration, but have a canned presentation as backup. In addition to a few examples that you know will produce results, take advantage of audience questions to show additional facets of the resource. As Chris Tovell (2001) says, "Search failure provides an excellent opportunity for classroom interaction and gives your more experienced colleagues an opportunity to share their knowledge." Give students a chance to work with the resource under your supervision, either at the training class or during additional sessions in the library.

"One of the more delicate situations information professionals face is tactfully training people who outrank us. Our superiors are used to being the experts. Having to admit they don't know something is hard on them; having to learn it from someone they outrank is even harder" (Block 2000c). Let them know that you realize they are the experts in the business or product, but that you provide the expertise in acquiring, organizing, and disseminating information. This establishes a partnership in achieving personal and organizational goals. Another way to approach this is to tell them you are not really teaching, just coaching. Because you use library products and services all the time, you are sure to know some tips and tricks that they have not discovered yet, and you have the time to locate new resources for them. Show them how to do more in less time, to find things faster or cheaper, or to find more information. Use illustrations of actual research questions—even solicit current problems from them ahead of time. Be ready for the unexpected and be able to improvise. Give them the logic behind what you show them—these kinds of people do not learn by rote but by understanding. Finally, make sure they have a deliverable to take with them—a cheat sheet, sample search, or list of websites—and emphasize that you are at the ready for additional instruction or troubleshooting.

## FEED THEM AND THEY WILL COME: OPEN HOUSES AND EXHIBITS

The open house can be a powerful PR tool. Food is the most important part of holding an open house; you *must* have food—lots of food. Chocolate is always appropriate, especially in the form of chocolate-chip cookies. Homemade ones are nice but not necessary; store-bought ones are quite satisfactory. Pizza is also good, especially when you want to attract men or teens. Don't place all the food in one place; you want attendees to circulate and see everything.

Start planning your open house well in advance of the event. Make sure the date does not conflict with other organizational or community events. Although you don't need an excuse to hold an open house or other form of a party, the calendar provides many good occasions to promote your library. Library associations in most countries sponsor a National Library Week; in the United States it is usually in April. The Special Libraries Association sponsors International Special Librarians Day during National Library Week. However, it is far better to hold your open house during a week or month that focuses on your customers. A hospital library could have its open house during Medical Library Month (October), but it would be even better to have one open house for doctors during Doctors Week, one for nurses during Nurses Week, one for lab personnel during Laboratory Technicians Month, and so on. The objective is to put the spotlight where it belongs—on your customers, not on the library.

Other occasions for an open house include an anniversary or milestone in the library or community, an autographing session featuring local or organizational authors, or bus tours to places of local historical interest that correspond with a special collection in your library. Product demonstrations are always popular. Invite vendors of databases, news feeds, books, or other library services to set up tables and present their products or services to your customers. There should be no problem getting the exhibitors to pay for a nice lunch or other refreshments, thereby providing better food at no cost to you.

Make sure that everyone in the organization or community knows about your open house. Use all the tips in chapter 3. Place posters on bulletin boards, in the cafeteria, near the rest rooms, or by the water cooler. I even put signs on the coffee machines saying, "Free Coffee This Morning in the Library." Send announcements or invitations to those people you especially want to attend, such as upper management, trustees, or local officials. To encourage them to attend, invite them to say a few words, cut a ribbon, or present them with an award or a small present. If you get a commitment from one of the "bigwigs," be sure to publicize this fact. Middle managers will attend if they know their boss will be there, and the rank and file will come if their bosses do.

Be sure to have enough handouts and giveaways for everyone. Hold a raffle or drawing; books make good prizes, but so do food baskets, free searches, or anything else that your customers will find of value. Place

---

### CASE STUDY

**THROWING A PARTY TO MEET ALL OF OUR PATRONS' NEEDS**
**Tunxis Community College**
**Farmington, Connecticut**

In 2001 the librarians at the Tunxis Community College in Farmington, Connecticut, had a party based on Maslow's Needs Hierarchy, using the library's mission statement: "We make your life easier." The theme was white and clinical and the library identified as "the place where all your needs are met." Hand delivered to 250 members of the administration, faculty, and staff, even maintenance, janitorial, and cafeteria workers, invitations were white prescription bags with a pyramid stapled to the outside with the words "You *belong* here!" Inside were a white stress ball with the library mission statement, a white fortune cookie with a library quote inside, white candy, a white pen, and white bookmarks. Posters that looked like the party invitations were placed in the main lobby of the school and outside the library to invite students. Inside the library were white balloons, twinkle lights, white tablecloths and napkins, white-chocolate- and vanilla-flavored coffees, a white soft-drink fountain, a white cake ("At the Tunxis Library, You Can Have Your Cake and Eat It Too!"), and all-white foods. The library staff wore white lab coats. Books featuring the various needs of Maslow's pyramid were highlighted in displays.

"In a theme-based party such as this, the focus was on meeting the needs of the patron, and none of us *(however exhausted)* strayed from that concept from start to finish." In addition to meeting the patrons' needs, the library's parties serve other functions: "Our unique events not only draw in the masses, but they also give us a means of breaking a few traditional library stereotypes: Here, people can talk in the library, be loud, eat, drink, and not see a single librarian wearing a button-down sweater or orthotic shoes" (Lavoie 2002, 2).

Results: most of the invitees and some students attended. Circulation went up during and for weeks following the party, and applications for new library cards and traffic increased (Lavoie 2002, 2).

a guest book or register near the entrance of the library to give you a record of attendees for after-event follow-up. I handed out stickers saying "I visited my library today." When attendees returned to their desks, others nearby saw the sticker and were reminded of the open house.

You do not have to do everything yourself. Delegate some tasks to your staff. Take advantage of the skills of other departments in your organization. Ask the graphics or marketing communications department to help with publicity or choosing giveaways. Ask someone else to take pictures so you can be the good host, appear in the pictures, and perhaps even enjoy yourself. Test computer equipment four to six hours before the open house starts to give you time to fix anything that does not work.

After the event, follow up. Send brochures or fliers to all attendees, visit departments or segments of the community that were not represented, and call selected attendees to get their ideas for improving future open houses. Post pictures taken at the event on the library bulletin board and on the website.

## THE PHYSICAL LIBRARY AS PUBLIC RELATIONS

> "Libraries are among the most complex and confusing of institutions accessible by the public: those not familiar with a particular library, even those who have used other libraries, can be bewildered by the building itself, the layout, the arrangement of the stock, the catalogues (especially), the various services offered, and even the staff (who are not generally distinguishable by uniforms as they are in stores or railway stations)." (Line 2002, 338–39)

Will a person coming into your library for the first time find a friendly and welcoming staff, informative signage, a logical layout? Can he or she find information without help? If help is needed, can a visitor find a librarian (or knowledgeable nonprofessional) without excessive searching? Will the experience be such that the person will want to come back? If you cannot answer these questions objectively, ask someone unfamiliar with the library (a family member or even a new employee) to come in and use the facility, perhaps even giving him or her some tasks to complete such as looking up an address or using one of the reference CD-ROM databases. Then act on the suggestions he or she makes.

### The Telephone

Some of your customers never enter the library at all—they call on the telephone.

When was the last time you called into your own library? Is the greeting friendly, accurate, and clear? It is better to have the telephone answered by a staff member, but if you use a recorded message with a voice-mail system, make sure it is easy to use and provides an option to reach a real person. Ask the caller's permission before putting him or her on hold, and wait to see if the answer to the question is yes or no. If it will be a while before you can get to the caller, go back on the line and inform the caller; ask if he or she wants to hold or could you take the customer's number and return the call. If you are calling your own library as a checkup, ask a question. Does the staff member who answers the telephone know the answer? If not, how long does it take for you to reach someone who does know? Are you transferred more than once? If you reach a message, is it short and to the point or are you caught in "voice-mail hell," where you are sent from one menu to another with no option to talk to a live person? Does the message sound professional yet friendly? "We are currently giving personal attention to another customer. Please hold, and we will be happy to provide the same for you" sounds better than "All staff are busy; please hold." When you are out of the library for a meeting, your message should be along the lines of "Today I am attending a workshop to learn new methods of providing you with excellent information delivery. If you leave a detailed explanation of your needs, I will be happy to help you as soon as I return." Such a message creates a better image than "I am away from my desk. Please leave a message." Never transfer a caller to another person unless you know that (1) the person is actually in and (2) the person can really handle the inquiry. Remember, the telephone may be the only contact a customer has with your library, and it must be a positive experience.

Here are some additional PR ideas from fellow librarians. Honor members of your community who have written books or articles or who have received awards. During Australian Library Week, the City of Perth Library took over the central railway station with an Internet display and handed out brochures to the general public. This generated a great deal of interest among passersby and enticed a number of people to try the Internet who would never have had the courage to enter the library. The Hewlett-Packard Library holds a "Coffee Schmooze" the first Monday of the month, complete with a gourmet coffee cart. They also have High Tea Talks in midafternoon with highly qualified speakers discussing such topics as copyright, news retrieval, patents, tacit knowledge, venture capital, and technology spin-offs. Related books are put on display, and a bibliography is handed out to attendees. These talks have "elevated the library image as a place that challenges and feeds employees' intellect" (Dworkin 2001, 53).

# WORD-OF-MOUTH PUBLIC RELATIONS

> "The other thing that is very important, and the only thing that really matters to librarians, is word-of-mouth publicity."
> (Scilken in Deitch 2002, 56)

> "Word of mouth can be managed. You are not merely at the mercy of those who talk. You can take control and use these ideas to put together your own word-of-mouth [PR] program."
> (Wilson 1991, ix)

Personal recommendations—or word of mouth—are very powerful, and people are much more likely to tell others about a bad experience than a good one. Positive word of mouth "is the result of hundreds of little things you consistently do a little bit better than your competition" (Wilson 1991, viii). Unfortunately, one bad experience can cause a customer to forget all the good things you have done. Therefore, you have to work very hard to make sure that people are saying only good things about you, your library, its staff, and its products and services. "You must have a good product or service to use word-of-mouth [PR] strategies—otherwise, you'll just be spreading bad news" (14). Bad service generates negative talk, good or adequate service generates no talk, but only great service generates positive talk. Make sure your service gives your customers no choice but to talk positively about your library. When you introduce a new product or service, plan a word-of-mouth PR campaign to generate positive word of mouth before the release. Doing so will blunt any negative experiences that may occur when the product or service actually debuts.

# OTHER PERSON-TO-PERSON PUBLIC RELATIONS METHODS

## The Elevator Speech and the Thirty-Second Commercial

Often you will have an impromptu opportunity to market your library, such as finding yourself in the elevator with someone you want to impress. Have a prepared "elevator speech" that has a beginning (to introduce yourself), a middle (the pitch), and an end (to request action, a meeting, or a visit). Start with a provocative statement or question such as "Did you know that 40 percent of an executive's time is spent looking for information?" Although your time is limited, don't speak too fast. Finally, practice, practice, practice.

The "thirty-second commercial" is similar to the "elevator speech" but is designed to tell a stranger who you are and what value you can bring him or her. For instance, "I am Judith A. Siess of Information Bridges International. I specialize in management information for small and solo libraries. I accomplish this by publishing *The One-Person Library* newsletter and presenting workshops around the world. I just finished writing my fourth book." The use of the phrases "solo libraries" and "fourth book" usually generate questions or comments and give me a chance to tell them more about me and my company.

## Cooperation and Teamwork

Libraries can be conservative and hierarchical organizations. In addition, many librarians prefer working in relative isolation. However, in the twenty-first century, hierarchy is out, and teams and networking are in. Working in teams improves the image of the library and its staff. Marilyn J. Flood offers ten suggestions for team success: "Respect the other players. Listen carefully to everyone's views. Be patient—about everyone and everything. Encourage honest and direct communication. Practice diplomacy. Trust the people and the process. Be loyal to the team. Maintain a sense of humor. Share bad news or problems immediately. Share good news and compliments immediately" (1999, 225–26).

What are some specific ways libraries can collaborate with other groups? A librarian in a museum works closely with curators, collection managers, researchers, and educators to create, document, and teach visitors about museum exhibits and collections. Corporate librarians can collaborate by sitting in on project planning meetings to offer suggestions on resources that may be helpful or locating examples of similar projects. A hospital library could work with the public library to provide consumer-health information or serve on health-related community committees. A public library can create displays in the library using items from local merchants, cosponsor an autograph party with a local independent bookstore, or work with a local hospital on a health fair.

## Public Relations for Specific Groups

### ACADEMIA

Your target audience consists of faculty, students, staff, alumni, prospective students, and, often, the surrounding community. Send a welcome packet to new faculty before they arrive on campus with a letter of congratulations and welcome, a list of library products and services, key library contact names, and—to provide that extra measure of service—local maps and services to help with their relocation. Once they are on campus, arrange an informal meeting to set up accounts and e-mail and to provide passwords and a library tour. Offer lunchtime seminars on new technologies. Offer student classes in research methods and reading clubs. Set up displays or exhibits outside the library—in the student union, dormitories, or the gym. The University of Illinois has satellite libraries in some of the dorms, staffed by professional librarians who offer research assistance. At one college, reference librarians meet with each section of the required Freshman Seminar and work with the students on research methods, catalog use, and article retrieval in periodical databases. Librarians tie coverage of library basics to the themes of the individual courses and create Web pages for each class with selected Web resources and a general tutorial that students can use for review (Gaynor 2002). Outreach to alumni and the community also enhances the reputation of the library. Use your Web page to offer your fee-based services to the community. Offer "associates" cards to the business community for a fee.

## CORPORATIONS

Make sure the library is included in new employee orientation or at least in their materials. At a minimum, each new employee should have the library's URL, location, hours, phone number, and e-mail address. Get a list of new employees and send them a welcome e-mail or information packet, complete with an invitation to a tour of the library. Create department- or function-specific handouts. Create a virtual library tour on the company intranet.

## HOSPITALS

Send a welcome letter to new staff, inviting them to visit the library. Attend Grand Rounds or continuing medical education (CME) sessions, and ask questions. Market the library to off-site physicians. Write for the medical staff newsletter or physician-only area of the hospital website. Have library brochures available at all CME activities.

# 5 Advocacy: Putting It All Together

"Doesn't everyone realize that today's librarians are technological wonders fighting evil while defending the premise of liberty and information for all? No, apparently they don't. So be afraid, be very afraid." (Dempsey 2002, 77)

"The [Minnesota] Department of Children, Families, and Learning (CFL) on June 4 [2002] gutted the Office of Library Development and Services (LDS) and transferred its central functions. . . . The state library collection was closed." "The Arkansas Board of Education reduced state aid to . . . a level little more than 10 percent of state funding two years ago. It could have been worse; the education department had recommended eliminating the whole State Aid to Public Libraries." The governor of Colorado used his line-item veto to cut library support by more than $4 million in $46 million of cuts statewide, eliminating all support for the statewide resource center at the Denver Public Library and a $2 million grant program for small rural libraries (Oder 2002, 14–15). These are just three examples of what is happening to public and state libraries in nearly every state. At the local level, library levies fail with frightening regularity. When the National Wildlife Federation built a new headquarters, there was no library included in the plans. (Luckily, the librarian retained her job, but her visibility was diminished.) Law firms reduce the space for the law library to add more offices. Add this to the constant downsizing or closing of corporate libraries and mergers of hospitals creating multiple libraries managed by one librarian and you have the invisible librarian.

## How Did We Get into This Mess?

For the most part, people have no clue what it takes to become a librarian, what a librarian does, and how librarians can help them. It would be nice to blame this on someone else, but, as Shakespeare's Julius Caesar said, "The fault, dear Brutus, is not in our stars, But in ourselves, that we are underlings" (*Julius Caesar,* Act I, Scene 2, Rows 140–41). What do we do that makes us invisible? "Only 20 percent of what we do is visible to other people" (Garcia 2000, 1). Our customers see us handling books, chatting with a customer, and enforcing rules. No one sees us reading reviews of newly published books so we can decide which to buy. No one sees us reading manuals for new software or following electronic discussions of which databases or search engines are the best for which questions. No one sees the catalogers struggling with a difficult book or CD that doesn't seem to fit into any one category. No one sees the interlibrary loan people searching for a hard-to-find article. No one sees the reference librarian searching five different databases to find that elusive fact. And no one sees the librarians in budget meetings or buttonholing politicians or management to try to get a few more dollars for the library.

In our quest to empower our users, we have buried the role of the librarian in information provision. We put more and more resources on websites or intranets—without making customers aware of what it took to get them there. Customers do not see the process of selection, negotiation for rights, creation of user-friendly interfaces, or maintenance of the online catalog and other resources. In addition, "We have sabotaged ourselves by failing to tell people that the databases we provide for them by way of the Internet may be free to them, but in fact are astoundingly expensive resources that only a library can afford to buy. If we don't emphasize that our databases are free only because we have paid the subscription fee, we may fall victim to the public perception that people don't need the library because, after all, all those wonderful databases are free on the net" (Block 2002c). With more remote services, fewer users visit the library and may forget what the *librarians* do for them. After all, if you can do it all yourself, why do you need a "high-priced" librarian?

Our own attitudes have hurt us, too. We make assumptions about our customers that just aren't true. "Most public libraries [and other types as well] currently make these assumptions about most of their users: they know what they are looking for; they'll ask if they can't find something; it doesn't matter if they don't find something this time, they will come back; [and] they come with all the time in the world" (Van Riel 2002, 38). One-person or solo librarians sometimes complain that they have so many interruptions that they can't get their work done, but if no one interrupted them, they wouldn't have jobs. Librarians are often much too passive. We are afraid to raise a fuss or to complain, lest we be thought to be whiners or even bitchy. Edward B. Stear said that because "the IRC [information resource center—another euphemism for *library*] only supplies information when it has been asked to . . . the IRC will forever be viewed as an 'extra' rather than as an integral part of the business—i.e., a strategic function" (1997, 26). We are a profession named after a building. We need to "market what goes on in that building, its content, and the rest [our image] will take care of itself" (Pace 2000, 64). Even our professional organizations have a perceptual problem. "The ALA [and SLA and AALL and MLA, etc.] advocate for libraries, not librarians. [Can you] imagine the American College of Operating Rooms?" (Graham 2002).

Finally, too few librarians have management skills and political savvy. For too long, we have felt that libraries are a given, a public good that will always exist. In one multitype library system, the librarians working in hospitals and public utilities seemed surprised that those of us who worked in corporate libraries were always concerned about our jobs—their jobs seemed so secure. Later, when the jobs of those hospital and utility librarians were being eliminated because of mergers and acquisitions, one newly downsized librarian said, "Now we understand how you felt." We also concentrate too much on saving money. "Saving money is *not* your job. Avoiding waste of money in information operations (yours and others in the corporation) *is* your job" (White 1984, 361). Herbert S. White said that "all librarians are ultimately judged, and rewarded or punished, through the awarding or withholding of resources by nonlibrarians, who do not necessarily share the concerns or understand the standards of librarians" (1984, 33). Librarians in law firms "believed that a lawyer would still come to us for most of his research needs. We were complacent about showing our value" (Ellis 1999, 28–29). Then Baker and McKenzie—the world's largest law firm—closed its library and outsourced its services. "We began to realize that possibly our value was not perceived by our employers" (29). Most librarians report to nonlibrarians who don't know much about libraries, and many don't care to know more. And even when we are supported in theory, we may not receive the funding we need. Support from management or the community must be accompanied by money or it is worthless. Although we may have learned in library school about preparing a budget, no one told us how difficult it would be to convince management to agree to it, and there were no courses on lobbying or advocacy.

## What Can We Do?

Enough moaning about our situation (something we as a profession do far too well and much too often). We must accept the situation as it is and move on. That is not to say that we shouldn't try to make things better, however. "As should now be abundantly clear, the greatest problem with management is not opposition but indifference" (White 1984, 104). We must convince management to care about the library and value what is done there and by whom it is done. Our first task is to make sure the library and its objectives are in alignment with the strategic objectives of the parent organization or community. Then we must decide what value the library creates for its customers and communicate that (our worth) to management, in their own language. Third, we must do whatever is necessary to make sure we get our share of the resources of the organization or community. Finally, we must learn to use marketing and advocacy effectively as tools to accomplish these goals.

## ALIGN THE LIBRARY WITH THE STRATEGIC OBJECTIVES OF YOUR CUSTOMERS

Sometimes the answer to "Why does the library matter?" is the economic value it brings to the user, and sometimes it is more abstract, such as improving the user's quality of life. Your goal is to make the library intimately involved in helping the organization (and its employees) or the community reach its goals. Does upper management consult with the library before undertaking a new project? Does the library manager have a say or input in organizational policy or planning? Are the decision makers in the community coming into the library on a regular basis? "The challenge to the information professional is clear: to create an information environment that ensures consumer access to dynamic intelligence mechanisms that can lead to 'smart' tactical and strategic decisions" (Kennedy 1996, 120).

## COMMUNICATE OUR WORTH

Most administrators do not know the costs or value of the libraries in their organization or community. "Organizations [or cities] do not know how much to spend for support services, and specifically for libraries. Since they do not know, the safest thing to do is cut" (White 1984, 359). When presenting your case to management, use techniques and terms that they understand. Using statistics and relatively simple calculations, show that the value of what you do easily meets or exceeds the amount spent on the library (including salary and benefits, the collection, subscriptions, online services, the physical plant, and utilities). One law librarian showed that she saved the law firm the cost of her salary and benefits simply by checking the invoices from the legal publishers. The law firm had been paying all of the invoices—duplicates and erroneous ones as well as the correct ones. Joan Shear wrote of "a court adminis-trator who gave his secretary a password to a commercial system and asked her to retrieve some documents for him. When she finally called the library for help, she had already run up a $32,000 bill. And the librarians actually knew how to get the same information without charge. The librarians worked with the online vendor to eliminate the huge bill in return for a mutually favorable contract for future usage" (2001, 30).

You have to be firm with management about money. Do not—repeat, do not—accept budget cuts without explaining to management the con-sequences of the cut. It is really very simple: no money, no service. One librarian was responsible for audiovisual (AV) services and one full-time AV staff member. The AV position was cut to half-time, and services were reduced. After six months or so, there were so many complaints that the position was reinstated to full-time. The lesson? When you must cut ser-vices, make sure that they are services that will be noticed, that will "hurt" someone. Cutting back office services will hurt no one except the already-overworked librarian. If you absorb cuts in budget or staff and nothing bad happens, management will (correctly) assume that you were overstaffed or had too much money. If you use a program budget instead of a line-item budget, they will have to cut a whole program to cut your budget.

In organizations, most libraries are considered overhead expense. This is not a very safe situation. When economic times are tough, man-agement looks first to eliminate overhead. Although you may not need to become a profit center, you are better equipped for survival if you at least break even. "The library cannot spend enough, no matter how extravagant we get, to affect earnings by even one cent per share" or to make even a ripple in the bottom line (White 1984, 344). "The public generally thinks libraries get more support than they do. . . . [The public library] runs on about 2 percent of local tax returns. Nobody is going to balance the budget on the backs of the local library . . . you don't cut library services to save money" (Scilken in Deitch 2002, 55). Therefore, to concentrate on money savings alone is not enough. "There is no safety in being cheap because we will never be cheap enough. Our safety lies in being essential" (White 1996b, 59). An important way the library can add value is its ability to increase or capitalize on the intellectual capital (knowledge, processes, contacts, experience) of an organization or com-munity. Testimonials from satisfied customers demonstrating specific money or time savings are also valuable. Make sure these testimonials are from people whose opinions carry weight in the organization or community.

This brings us to a very important point. You can calculate the financial and intellectual value of the library all you want, but if management does not know about it, you are still doomed. "Only when the information center has strong advocates within itself and in other areas of the organization will it be able to thrive and grow. Just as in Congress, where resource allocation decisions are made on the basis of which coalition or interest group presents the most compelling cause, so too in the workplace [or community]. The voices which are the strongest will prevail" (Jones in St. Clair 1994, xiv).

When preparing reports for management or library trustees, "don't report what management neither understands nor cares about" (White 1984, 100–101). The report should be short and easy to read. "The main thrust of the report must be the statement of accomplishments and problems. Accomplishments should not reflect inwardly on the library, but on the contribution to the units being served. . . . Traditional measures of library services, such as counting interlibrary loans or keeping track of reference questions answered, does not mean much to the average corporate executive [or city council or library board]. . . . They need to be interpreted to demonstrate their value." Finally, "as [Peter] Drucker has often noted, the essence of management communication is exception reporting—stressing not what good things are happening but what good things are *not* happening" (White 1997, 117).

> The first ally we want is the local power structure. Do librarians know what their mayors' [CEOs', presidents'] pet projects are, and supply them with a steady stream of books, articles and information about how other towns are accomplishing the same things? Do they regularly route information to the city manager, the police chief, the aldermen, the editor of the local newspaper, the head of the Chamber of Commerce? If not, why not? There's nothing like meeting people's needs before they even know they have them to make them realize that librarians—not the bookstores, not the net, not the commercial services that are trying to provide for a fee the same services we do—are the go-to people for information. Business leaders [faculty, executives, researchers] need to be reminded how much information librarians give them to enable their decision-making. We need to point out to them that, though there's an overwhelming amount of pertinent information on the net, librarians know how to *find* it and sort through it. (Block 2000b)

## MAKE SURE WE GET THE RESOURCES WE NEED—AND DESERVE

How often have you been asked to add a service without being given the money or staff to do so? Public librarians are very familiar with such "unfunded mandates" as requirements for ramps and elevators as a consequence of governmental regulations. However, other kinds of libraries receive requests (or sometimes orders) to provide new services without the resources needed to implement them. This is when you need all the management support you can muster. Stear (1997) outlines ten ways to get management support:

1. "Express expected results in terms that people can understand and judge."
2. "Understand the project in business terms and express it that way."
3. "Understand the big picture and present it. Calculate and illustrate the ripple effect that the target project has on the whole enterprise."
4. Frame your request as a way to improve the organization or community's ability to compete.
5. "Frame the project in the context of corporate [or community] objectives."
6. "Relate the project to an internal condition" such as downsizing, employee turnover, loss of jobs or workers in the community.
7. "Relate the project to an external condition that requires a response."
8. "Completely understand customer requirements."
9. "Ask at least two key or favored vendors to provide equipment, software, and support for the pilot [project] at no cost."
10. Ask a colleague who's been successful to talk to your boss.

This brings us to a critical concept—the library champion. "Win the backing of at least one strong person in the organization, preferably at the management level" (Williamson 1996, 3). However, one is definitely not enough; you need all the supporters you can get, at as high a level as you can find. When there is a question of continued support for the library, or the competence of its staff or quality of its products or services, your champions can stand up and fight for you and your library. At budget time, you can go to them and say, "Look, we seem to be doing a good job for you, but with a little help and a little more money, we could really show you service!" (Evans, Ward, and Ruggas 2000, 443). Then ask them to help you get it. Faculty (and students, although their voices may not have as much clout) have been enlisted to help save funding for a campus library.

How do you find or cultivate champions? Champions must be more than just frequent users. Not only must they be willing to work with and for you, they must also have influence with upper management. Let them know that their support is critical to the library's continued ability to help them and the institution. Make it easy for them to help you by suggesting exactly what they can say and to whom. Let them know how much you appreciate their help by thanking them personally and or publicly. Additional sources for champions are library boards, friends groups, and trustees. Work with these ready-made champions; get them involved, get their approval, use their influence to get speaking engagements, and get them to lobby for you. Draw on people within the organization who are involved in planning or oversight of knowledge activities or even outsiders such as clients (very effective in law firms) or suppliers, vendors, and professional colleagues. Public libraries can draw on local authors and other highly literate (and visible) members of the community.

Here is an example of a good supporting statement by a library champion. "The public library is our town's R&D department. It is an investment we simply can't afford to neglect" (an elected selectman of a small New England town, in Berry and Wilson 2001, 6). Or this one by a computer consultant: "Librarians [have] been managing complex information for over 200 years. If we were smart, we'd let librarians rule the net" (Schneiderman 1997, 34–35). Librarians would have insisted on better indexing, identification, and classification of Web information. End-users primarily search by keywords, which often fails miserably when searching the Web. They would make sure that "every document would have at least been identified by author, title, date, and a subject heading." Moreover, if librarians were running the Internet, "It would have given us a fighting chance of finding the information we really need. . . . In the long run, the only way the Net will rise to its true potential is if librarians become an integral part of the discussion of the Net's future. In the meantime, we need to fight to make sure that libraries survive and thrive in the new Information Age, and we need to start giving librarians the respect they are due."

## USE MARKETING AND ADVOCACY EFFECTIVELY

"Advocacy . . . might be thought of as a process in which those who are in a position to affect the delivery of library services, whether as users, management or interested observers, are targeted as supporters for the library." (St. Clair and Williamson 1992, 66)

Many librarians do not feel comfortable acting as advocates for themselves. Others think that our professional associations will do the job. However, the American Library Association and many other library associations around the world focus their marketing on *libraries*. Even those that focus more on the library professional still carry it out mostly in the library- or information-related media, not in the business or management media. We need articles and, even better, advertisements showing the value of information professionals in *Time, Fortune, Business Week,* and the *Harvard Business Review* and interviews with librarians and library champions on *Wall Street Week* and the *Nightly News.* (As of the time this book was written, some baby steps were being taken in this direction. *Inc.* magazine has a column written by an "information posse" of corporate librarians, and at least one advertisement has appeared in some major U.S. magazines highlighting Eugenie Prime, a librarian at Hewlett-Packard. However, the *Inc.* column is relatively light fare, and the Prime ad still shows her surrounded by books and looking more like an old-fashioned librarian than I know Eugenie to be.)

We can no longer sit back and wait for someone else to decide our own information futures. We must decide what we want our future to be and take all the actions we can to make sure it unfolds in the way we desire. "Any librarian who claims not to have the time to build support for his or her library [is] committing 'political suicide'" (Finch in Kirchner 1999, 844). If the resources you need are not coming to you, they must be going to someone else. Your task is to make such a compelling case for allocating resources to your library that the decision makers have no alternative but to do so.

It is commonly said that knowledge is power. Librarians already have the knowledge; now we must acquire the power. "Librarians do not usually set out to be manipulators or wielders of power; they want to provide a service, the value of which they see as self-evident, and they expect others to be able to see it too" (White 1984, 85). Power is not the same as influence. "Influence is the ability to use examples or actions to cause others to change their behavior. Power is the ability to do something. Authority is the right to do something" (Evans, Ward, and Ruggas 2000, 194).

> How often do you use all the opportunities for promotion to make a politically powerful case for your library? Do you ensure that every time you inform your public about library services you also let them know why it matters? And not just why it

matters in general (i.e., libraries are good), but why libraries matter to everyone in the community, even those who don't use the library. Being an effective advocate for libraries may be one of the most important roles for today's librarian. It is no longer a role that can be successfully played once a year at budget time; it must become a part of everything we do, every message we send. These are exciting and perhaps even scary times, but if you became a librarian to make a difference, the opportunity to do so has never been greater. (Reed 2001, xiii–xvii)

Despite what you may think, *politics* and *lobbying* are not dirty words but necessities in every organization. But you must use the political process effectively. Make sure both you and your library have credibility with the decision makers. Anticipate any opposition or negatives and have a response prepared. Keep lines of communication open. Court the decision makers; send them updates throughout the year. Understand the players—those for and against you. Don't forget the staffers who prepare the decision makers.

Sometimes nothing works. Is it time for drastic action? We complain about poor salaries and lack of status. What would happen if "*no* librarian would accept less than an appropriate salary, benefits, and status" (Adams 2002)? This is nice in theory but is very unlikely to work. Someone would always be willing to make the sacrifice, and some organizations really cannot afford to pay more. Here's another, more radical idea.

To observe National Library Week, close the libraries. Send library workers on strike. Use the time off to lobby local jurisdictions for more money. When students are unable to complete their assignments, when businesspeople can't get the information they need (and no, it's *not* all on the Internet), when investors can't get access to the latest issue of *Morningstar* or *ValueLine* and—particularly at tax time—when people can't get the tax forms they need, perhaps *then* we can find people who will bankroll the petition-gathering campaign and the advertising to support the [funding] initiative. (Kamm 2002)

Even former administrator Herbert S. White has a drastic solution. When budget cuts cut service, we should let questions pile up and lines form—and let the media see it so as to embarrass the funders. We'd either get fired or they'd do something about the problem (1997).

---

### CASE STUDY

## STORY OF A SUCCESSFUL REFERENDUM CAMPAIGN
### Indian Trails Public Library District
### Wheeling, Illinois

Indian Trails Public Library District, Wheeling, Illinois, passed their tax-increase referendum on the first try. How did they do it? First, they hired a coordinator to keep everyone "on task and all on the same page." Second, they did not use staff to make calls or ring doorbells, so that staff could "devote all their energy to providing the level of service that we hoped we would be able to continue." Next, all board members "delivered the same message in the same way: We haven't had a tax increase for operating funds since 1975. You want more of everything, and we want to provide it for you." People don't want to hear about the details, just "to know what it will cost, in the simplest terms possible. Our board told them so simply and directly that they were believed." They got the support of the local newspapers and the president of the village board. Board members spoke everywhere, went door-to-door. "Every weekend for months, a pair of board members in distinctive and tasteful polo shirts established a presence in the library lobby, and every patron who went by got a short spiel and the offer of a flyer. It was every patron, because those board members were not content to sit at a table and wait politely to be approached. They shrewdly placed a large bowl of candy on the table, and when children spotted it, and dragged their parents over, the parents got the spiel and the flyer." They also spoke at the beginning of all library programs and made phone calls (Smith 2002, 14).

---

## *Advocacy Ideas for Specific Types of Libraries*

### MEDICAL LIBRARIES

A hospital library can save money for the institution by decreasing costs caused by negative patient outcomes by providing rapid access to up-to-date information; decreasing the cost of continuing education through in-house resources such as journals, videos, and websites; decreasing the cost of obtaining information for research and decision making through membership in consortia; attracting and retaining better candidates for medical staff (who expect access to good on-site library services); decreasing the cost of acquiring information through centralized purchasing and eliminating of duplicate subscriptions; and decreasing the hidden costs of nonproductive time spent in looking for information (searches and document delivery) (Hammond and Priddy 2001).

## CASE STUDY

### RISING FROM THE ASHES (TWICE)
### Richmond Heights Hospital
### Richmond Heights, Ohio

Carol M. Shisler started as a one-person librarian (OPL) during a time of low staff morale and low budgets. "If the library was to survive, it was imperative that the library be seen as a vital part of the organization" (2000, 251). She created an action plan. First, develop a new image. She devised a new logo, which she put on everything that left the library. Then she began to establish open communications with potential or key users, via a newsletter, an annual report, a survey, and attending meetings. She talked to physicians, nursing and allied health, administration, patients, and families.

She concentrated her marketing on physicians because they were the heaviest users. The library was viewed as the doctors' library; "A major concern was that physicians would view any changes in library operations as a decline in services available to them." She needed to reassure them as well as provide faster turnaround time. "A clinical librarian service was initiated for residents who presented and attended morning report in the hospital. Follow-up materials were provided to all residents and students. A copy was sent to the medical director as well" (252).

She also marketed to nurses and other staff. Shisler talked to nursing department coordinators to see what they needed. She found that many of the nurses were not able to come to the library, so she moved a small core nursing collection to the nurses' lounge. She also centralized patient education materials in the library, with the librarian maintaining them; attended weekly nursing rounds; and added to the collection.

Shisler also marketed to patients, their families, visitors, and the community. She was asked to evaluate patient education materials in the emergency room. The library became a clearinghouse for all patient information materials. She created a catalog of materials and disseminated them to all physicians and all departments with an invitation to come to the library. In addition, Shisler contacted the public libraries and made a presentation at the regional library group and was asked by the nursing director to chair the Patient/Family Education Advisory Committee.

She requested that she report to the chief operating officer rather than the medical director. "The move positioned the library in the center of the institution" (252). In addition, she sought requests from the administrators and filled them rapidly.

The results of her efforts? Loans increased, searches tripled, support for the library increased from all departments—the library survived despite administrative changes, job cuts, and budget cuts.

Unfortunately, the success didn't last. The hospital itself nearly closed, saved only by being acquired by another hospital. In the meantime, the library had been closed, and Shisler moved on.

The library remained unstaffed for eight months, until Cathy Marshall was hired (again, a solo librarian). Volunteers helped out, but the collection had been "looted," leaving only out-of-date books in a dingy and crowded facility (2002). Marshall immediately began a process of reestablishing the library. She convinced the hospital management to remodel the library, and it is now a well-organized, bright, and cheery place. The collection is smaller now, with only about 500 books and 80 or so print journal subscriptions, but Marshall has added access to more than 250 online journals through the hospital's affiliation with a large hospital group. With a grant from a medical foundation (cowritten with two physicians), she was able to install six computer workstations, a television, and a video recorder in the library. There is now an online circulation system.

There is now almost constant traffic through the library. More of the hospital staff are aware of the presence of Marshall and the library. This is primarily because she has served on many committees and attended meetings dealing with medical education, standards of performance, and customer satisfaction. She participates in the maintenance and content of the hospital website as well.

Marshall has begun producing a library newsletter, in both paper and electronic form. It is posted in staff lounges and in the cafeteria and contains announcements of new products. She has placed an article in the hospital newsletter.

After a little more than a year on the job, Marshall has been able to return the Richmond Heights Hospital library to its former ability to serve its customers. Let's hope it lasts this time.

## LAW LIBRARIES

If the lack of billable hours becomes an issue for the law firm librarian, find out how many nonbillable hours the attorneys spend looking for information and point out how the librarian can cut this time. Track the hours you spend on practice development. Remind management that your work allows others to perform more billable work.

Terri Lawrence of Thompson and Knight LLP is described as "an experienced and successful law firm 'rainmaker' (i.e., a generator of legal business)." Because survival at a law firm may depend on generating new business, she monitors client legal and business activity, checks court docket records for litigation involving current and potential clients, prepares dossiers on selected clients, identifies cross-marketing possibilities, and supplies competitive information to the attorneys. She also helps the client development department find new methods to make its research better and finds and suggests business opportunities directly to the partners. "This is unusual and incredibly valuable" according to the director of client development (Shuck 2002, 4–5).

## BECOMING INDISPENSABLE TO YOUR ORGANIZATION: AVOIDING LIBRARY CLOSURES

Not a month goes by that we don't hear of the closing of another library. There is no reason to expect that this will not continue to occur as organizations and communities continue to downsize to decrease costs. Librarians have not been successful in dispelling the widespread but mistaken idea that "everything is available on the Internet, and it's all free."

Be proactive! "Don't wait to be asked to do something. Study your clients, find out what they need to do their jobs, and hand it to them on a silver platter before they even realize they need it" (Dempsey 2002, 79). One medical librarian describes herself as "a shameless self- and library-promoter." She tries to send her manager something of interest at least once a week and sends "regular reports to the Board, which to my knowledge none of our other departments does." She also uses the media to advance her cause, finding "a reason to send something to the newspapers monthly if not weekly" and does television interviews as often as possible (Weaver 2002).

The perception of reality is sometimes more important than reality itself. What management (or the taxpayers) think is true is more important than what really is true. This means that even if you are doing a super job, even if your users think you walk on water, it isn't enough if those in a position to decide the future of the library (those at the highest levels of management or voters who don't use the library) don't think you are worth the cost. Outsourcers may approach corporate executives or city government saying, "Outsource your library to us and we'll save you money." Make sure that your funders are so convinced of your worth that they tell the outsourcer, "Sorry, we're not interested in talking to you. You couldn't possibly do a better job than our wonderful library staff."

However, you can use outsourcing yourself to deal with rising costs or decreasing staff. One librarian found that she and her library "should move out of the business of providing high-volume, repetitive *transactional* services. These services can take a substantial amount of professional and administrative time" but actually add very little value. They began to outsource "commodity services" such as cataloging, document delivery, and current awareness (Lemon 1996). Outsource short-term projects that would otherwise require adding to the staff or nonprofessional tasks like updating legal loose-leaf services. Management likes outsourcing functions that result in an improvement in the bottom line, but be cautious lest management get the idea that it could outsource *all* of the library functions. Make sure that you are in control of the decision to outsource or not and what is to be outsourced.

Look at downsizing, or the decrease in library staff, as an opportunity to make changes to keep from becoming stale, to energize staff, to find new markets and users, to develop new products, and, most importantly, to improve the perception and image of the library and its staff and as an occasion for rethinking the mix of library products and services. Perhaps some of them can be outsourced or even eliminated. Labor-intensive but strategic services such as current awareness or tables of contents might be more efficiently outsourced or automated. Above all, don't let downsizing get you down. "Nobody looks forward to the prospect of downsizing, but when it's inevitable, the best thing you can do is maintain a positive attitude and keep right on marketing" (Edwards in La Rosa 1992, 58). Focus on what you *can* do, not on what you *can't*. You have to work smarter. Your users may need you even more now, because they too may have fewer resources available to do their work.

## PROFESSIONALISM: IT'S MORE THAN A SUIT

> "Are we concerned that in the absence of enough professional librarians something bad might happen? In the absence of enough professional librarians something bad *better* happen!" (White 1996a, 127)

Our image, as the title of this section says, is more than the way we dress. However, appearance does matter. We all know about the librarian stereotype: a tweed jacket or some other dowdy style, long skirts, orthopedic shoes, hair in a bun, and glasses. Unfortunately, a lot of librarians actually look like this. Even corporate librarians, in their effort to "blend in" with the predominantly suit-clad male establishment, fail to show any sense of style. We should dress appropriately for our situation. In some organizations that does mean a suit (and tie for men), but that does not mean we cannot be up-to-date and fashionable. In other organizations appropriate may mean something very different.

> The coat is a symbol of authority. Whether it is a lab coat, a business coat or other type, the person who wears a coat has some appearance of the cloak of authority. Clothes need to accent the individual, and not demand attention away from the librarian herself. Invest in some good clothes, well tailored. Style is not as important as a "good look" for you as an individual. Children's librarians are a class apart. What is needed is clothing that invites children to sit in your lap and can be comfortably worn while sitting on the cold floor during story hours. Surprisingly, the blue jeans look doesn't go well in this area. . . . The reason for this conundrum is that parents will too often consider a blue-jeans-clad children's librarian as a free baby-sitter, and are inclined to impose on her time and personal space. (Hadden 2002)

Another characteristic of professionalism is leadership. Leadership can be learned, although some people are more attitudinally predisposed to it than others. While management is the process of implementing objectives, leadership deals with vision and motivating people. Leaders see beyond the day to day, constantly reach out beyond their specific area, have strong political skills, and don't accept the status quo. Leaders are flexible. They allow others to exercise creativity in getting the job done and are willing to accept and even encourage failure because anyone can meet low goals; failure means goals are set high enough (Barter 1994). A reminder: you do not have to be a manager to be a leader. You can lead others, even those above you in the hierarchy, by example. Your leadership stems from what you do and how you do it, not from your job title. Leaders must also think longer term: think beyond today's problems, think beyond the library, think beyond librarianship, understand people, think politically, and think not about what is but what might be.

## Lifelong Learning: An Essential Part of Professionalism

> "Only through a continual process of self-development can the . . . librarian maintain professional competence and meet the challenge of change." (Buchanan 2000, 126)

It was never really true that once you had your library degree you could be an effective librarian "forever" without any further training except what you picked up on the job, but it certainly was easier in the past than it is now. The fast pace of change in modern society, in technology, in management theory and techniques, and in the subject matter of our libraries makes it imperative for librarians to continue the educational process throughout their lives. To survive in our rapidly changing world, one must be a perpetual student. One of the best ways is to attend professional development workshops and in-house training.

Lifelong learning or continuing education (CE) consists of on-the-job training, provided by the organization for its employees, and personal professional development—personal: "relating primarily to the needs of the individual, not the employing organization"; professional: contributing "to competence in the conduct of our vocation"; and development: the "dynamic continuous process of growth and achievement" (Bryant 1995, 1). In most cases, librarians will have to determine their own CE needs, arrange for workshops or classes, and probably pay for it themselves. Few employers or professional associations require CE. Although most professional associations offer courses at their annual conferences and some courses are offered on a regional or local level, we are still responsible for finding these resources.

What do we need to learn and how can we learn it?

*Organizational culture:* observe the organization, talk to others, read whatever in-house documents you can find.

*Management, including financial management:* take courses offered by library conferences or local or regional associations, business schools, or management professional associations. Read some of the many excellent management books available. Observe others to see both good and bad examples of management.

*Communication and presentation skills:* try courses from private vendors or communications or speech departments of local colleges and universities.

*Information technology:* contact your institution's computer department or consult the Web for courses from major software vendors. Don't forget courses from library schools and training offered at a very low cost by library automation and database vendors.

*Library and information skills, including knowledge management, research methods, and the information audit:* these are available from library schools, many via the Internet. Library associations also offer courses at their conferences, in regional locations, or though self-directed learning.

*Networking:* this is best learned on your own, by doing it, but there are books on the subject in most bookstores. See the "Sources

Cited" and "Additional Resources" sections of this book for suggestions.

*Subject knowledge:* you can learn this on the job from your customers or at in-house seminars or sit in on courses at your local college or university.

*Personal development skills, such as assertiveness, time management, and dealing with problem people:* there are good and low-cost courses offered by private companies, and courses are also offered at library conferences. There are also many good books available on these topics.

There are many informal opportunities to continue your education. You can learn a lot just by walking around your institution or community and observing and asking questions. Electronic lists on the Internet provide a constant stream of new resources—books, software, and databases—complete with evaluations. Professional conferences provide opportunities to talk to colleagues and exchange ideas and solutions.

How does CE help you? You learn new skills or update existing ones. Further education may improve your status within your organization, such as by acquiring certification as a computer network administrator. Participation in in-house education programs can help make others more aware of the library—and the librarian. You are certain to meet someone new at CE programs, thus widening your network of contacts. Some benefits are direct, such as increased efficiency or learning something that will save money, while others are more indirect. Education reenergizes you, increasing your morale and motivation and helping avert stagnation. "Mastering new technologies and other developments in the field also promotes job satisfaction and enhances leadership skills" (Hubbard 2002, 604).

"Continuing education for the professional staff members should be a normal part of any library's budget" (White 1984, 48). It *should* be, but it often isn't, and if it is, it is one of the first things cut in an economic crisis. James B. Casey (2002) writes that at his public library, 68 percent of the budget is for salaries and benefits (about the national average), yet only 1.6 percent is for staff development (dues, conferences, tuition reimbursement, in-service training, recruitment expenses). But this budget is rarely exceeded. Is this because 1.6 percent is all that is needed or because the staff has been accustomed to expecting only this small sum? If others are receiving funding, you should receive it as well.

Many librarians are unwilling to pay for CE or, more often, professional conferences. They won't go unless their employer pays. If your boss won't pay for the conference, does this relieve you of your professional obligations? Of course not. Because your boss obviously doesn't respect your professionalism, you should be updating your skills so you can look for a position where you will get that respect. You can't afford *not* to invest in your professional future. Prepare a list of conference events that you plan to attend. List receptions as "networking" opportunities, because that is what they really are. List the vendors that you deal with that are going to be there and the questions you can answer by talking with them. Provide a list of specific questions or information goals you plan to pursue at the conferences. Then, go back to your boss. Offer to split the cost or ask for the time off with pay. One year my boss asked me what I would do if he didn't pay for the conference. I said I would pay for it. What if he didn't give me time off? I said I would take vacation. What if he didn't let me take the vacation time? I said I would quit. He paid for the conference and gave me time off—he was just seeing if I was committed to the conference and not just interested in a paid vacation. (Believe me, a professional conference is *not* a vacation. You are "on" from 7:30 A.M. to 11:00 P.M.—or later. If our bosses could see how hard we work at conferences, we would never be turned down again.) Just remember to show your boss how the organization or community will benefit from your attendance at the conference. When you return from the conference, write a trip report. Emphasize what you learned that will benefit the organization or community and make you a more valuable employee. If you went to a formal CE class, include a copy of the completion certificate. Include the conference in your monthly and annual reports and show how your work has improved since the conference.

Don't limit yourself to meetings of your own professional association. Try a local meeting of another association; attend a meeting of your own association, but in a different part of the country; or go to a meeting or conference that your customers attend. Carol Ebbinghouse has two additional—wonderful—suggestions. "If you really want to learn about something new, commit to write an article [or book] on the subject, research the heck out of it, and submit it [for publication]" (2002b, 114). "If you already know everything on a subject, offer to teach it to others!" (115). You'll learn as you teach.

Many of us became librarians because we like to read. Turn this love of reading into lifelong learning. What should you be reading? First of all, read all the publications of any professional organizations to which you belong. This includes the news items, book reviews, personnel changes, and, of course, the articles, even if they are not in your field. "Ask 10 of your forward-thinking customers what they are reading and why. Your customer will likely be shocked at your interest. You may even learn of topic areas that you should collect for your library" (Hurst 2002,

73). Ask other librarians what they are reading. Read a library publication outside of your own area to get a different perspective. *Library Journal* provides a good overview of the library world although it is heavy on public and academic libraries. The *Journal of Hospital Librarianship* is wonderful—even for librarians outside the medical field. *Church and Synagogue Libraries* has wonderful columns and articles on how to do a lot with no money. If you work in business, read the *Wall Street Journal* and the *Harvard Business Review*. Read what your customers read. "Read the reviewing media your readers read" (Scilken in Robinson 2002, 34). Subscribe to at least one electronic discussion list. I suggest SOLOLIB-L (for anyone, not just one-person librarians), LIBREF-L, BUSLIB-L, or MEDLIB-L. If these don't suit you, go to <http://www.liszt.com> and find one that you like.

"How will I ever find time to read all that?" you ask. I skim everything (tables of contents, headlines, captions under pictures, e-mail subject lines) first. If it is a short article I read it right away. If it is longer, I put it by my easy chair and read it later. I tear out the interesting articles, websites to check on, or books I want to order. As for e-mail, what I read depends on the subject, the sender, and how much time I have. I use an e-mail program that lets me make folders for each area that I'm interested in and use filters to send posts into the folders. Why do I read so much? I read because I am a professional and that means keeping up with my profession. It is one of my most important forms of continuing education.

## Networking: An Essential

> "No matter how smart you are, no matter how talented, you can't do it alone. You need a network. You need *your* network. Every day. A network will help you deal with some of life's minor annoyances as well as your most challenging problems." (Mackay 1997, 11)

Perhaps the most important weapon in a librarian's arsenal is his or her personal network of colleagues. We are very lucky to be working in a profession where helping others extends to helping other librarians as well. When we have a sticky question, we know that we can call a colleague or post it on a library discussion list. Within a few minutes or hours, we will have the answer—sometimes, many answers.

To put it simply, a network is everyone you know who can help you or who you can help. Harvey Mackay could have been describing librarians when he wrote, "Superior technical networkers are the ones who:

dial up the best people in their specialty to get an answer when they are stuck with a problem [and] are most likely to be confided in by their peers and are therefore likeliest to become 'hubs' [gatekeepers] in their disciplines" (1997, 13). The essential features of a network are reciprocity: "You give; you get. You no give; you no get" (65); mutual aid: sharing what you know with others to whom it would benefit; and freely sharing: helping others without expecting something in return.

Networks require constant attention and maintenance. You need to stay in touch with your networking partners so that you do not forget them and vice versa. You may have to give information to someone for a long time before he or she reciprocates with something worthwhile, but it will happen eventually. If you need help finding a new job or a job in a new area, use your network. Your network can also make you look good by extending your resources to include those of all the members of your network. The more people you have in your network and the more diverse they are, the better. "Don't build a network that looks just like you" (Mackay 1997, 177). A network can even save money. You can find someone who needs a product or service that you have and trade for a product or service of his or hers. Finally, and this is very important, always thank the people you contact, even if they are of no help; they may be able to help next time. Never take your contacts for granted.

*Networking* is an active rather than a passive verb. Go to trade group meetings, professional societies, and local meetings; go to national conferences; attend CE events—not only do you learn something new, but you also meet new people. Become active in some organization—professional or otherwise. Professional associations provide you with a ready-made network. Don't forget the Internet; you can make excellent contacts through e-mail and electronic discussion lists. Be aware that men and women network differently. Men's networking is more business oriented, while women are more interested in compatibility. Women share personal details; men don't. Women talk about their children; men don't. Men network through sports; women don't. Recruit successful or powerful people for your network, but don't limit your network to the powerful. "Cultivate relationships with administrative assistants [and secretaries, especially the boss's] who know what's going on before anyone else" (Kassel 2002, 3). To this I would add the people in the mail room and the receptionist.

A network, like any other tool, requires maintenance. You cannot possibly remember the name of everyone you have met, so creating a networking database is essential. It doesn't matter what form the database takes. As Mackay says, "It is a lot like getting dressed in the morning. It doesn't matter so much *how* you do it, it just matters *that* you do it" (Mackay 1997, 128). You can keep your contact information on file cards or in a Rolodex, but a computer database provides more access points. It resolves questions such as "I remember his name was John, but not the last name . . ." or "Do I file this business card under his name or his company?" or "Now who was that red-haired woman who spoke so eloquently about filtering at last month's council meeting?" Your networking database should include fields for name, title (Ms. or Mrs., Ph.D., M.D., Alderman, Director, etc.), organization, address, voice and fax numbers, e-mail address and URL, birth date (so you can call to say "Happy Birthday"), connections (where you met, common interests or organizations to which you both belong, friends in common or who referred you to the person), family (spouse's name or partner or significant other, children with their ages or year of birth, significant pets), education (alma maters, majors, fraternities), other affiliations (church, synagogue, service clubs), special interests (dog breeder, president of a local club), significant career history (jobs held and where), and accomplishments (awards, special professional talents, publications). A contact database is of no worth unless it is used. Consult it before you call someone, to remind you of his or her details and to see what you talked about last time. After you have finished the call, update that person's record with any new information (married, divorced, children, new job). Periodically, call those in your database to touch base, update their information, and remind them you exist. Be sure to call them when *your* information changes so they can update *their* databases. You can also stay in touch with your network by sending cards for birthdays and holidays; calling or writing when you hear of job changes, promotions, or marriages; sending a clipping whenever they are mentioned in the newspaper or a journal; calling or visiting when someone is ill, out of work, or just down; and by attending weddings or graduations, if invited, and funerals.

## *Creating Your Own Job Satisfaction: Career Planning*

"When work engages us, it is rewarding. We feel challenged, not swamped. We're motivated because we are enjoying what we are doing, regardless of the actual task involved. Chronic stress, pressure, and deadlines, with no hope of improvement in the foreseeable future, can lead to the exhaustive state we refer to as burnout" (Tomlin 1999, 10). Perhaps you are having trouble with your manager. It is difficult being managed and evaluated by nonlibrarians. Are you having trouble getting the employees of your organization or the members of your community to take full advantage of your products and services? Is turnover—of library staff or your customers—becoming a problem? Or are you just plain burned out? Do you feel angry or unhappy at work? Are you taking more sick or "mental health" days than you used to take? Are you tired at the end of the day even though you didn't do much? Is the quality of your work slipping? Are you reluctant to try anything new? Burnout can be caused by too much work to do with too few staff, too little money, and too little time. Answering the same questions or performing the same tasks over and over leads to boredom, and boredom leads to burnout. The increasingly rapid pace of change, especially in technology, also takes a toll, as does our lack of time for training on new technology and the amount of time we spend coordinating and troubleshooting computers.

How can librarians prevent or cope with burnout? The best technique is humor. Don't take yourself and your job so seriously. Try to take some time off and do something you really enjoy, take a vacation, or try something you've never done before. Focus on your interests outside of work or concentrate on your relationships with family or friends. Australians have the right idea; after ten years in a position, employees earn three months "long service leave." Possibilities for a sabbatical are internships or fellowships, job exchanges, organization of or participation in professional conferences or workshops, community service or volunteer work, travel, and study or research. Time off can allow you to reaffirm your own professional focus, broaden your perspective, energize yourself, and reduce stress.

If you are considering a job change, keep a work journal. For one day, write down everything you do, think, and feel. Start when you get up in the morning—do you want to go to work? How do you feel when you get to the library? What should you do first? What *do* you do first? If they aren't the same, why? Note when you are doing things you like— what are they? How do you feel doing them? Do the same with things you dislike. After you finish, put the journal away for a week. After you can look at that day from a distance, read and analyze it. Make a list of those things that cannot be changed (structural and bureaucratic elements) and a list of those that can (personal and professional). Put at least one suggestion for change next to each of the latter. Then decide if you can live with those things you cannot change and if you have the will to change the others. Think hard about changing jobs. Would a new job be that much better or just different?

If you decide to stay with your current job, start acting on each of. the suggestions you wrote down. Sometimes just doing something about your situation will make you feel more in control and, therefore, happier and more satisfied. "Take an active role in seeking change since to 'wait around for superiors or fate [will] increase your sense of being power-less'" (Bardwick 1986, 172–73).

> Take a break; learn something new, change your attitude—quit feeling sorry for yourself, talk to other librarians—you are probably not alone, volunteer for a project, run for office, or write a paper. The activity will distract you from your frustration and success will give you confidence and motivation. Find an activity outside your career to alleviate any sense of disappointment or frustration that you may feel with your employment situation. Finally, do not let yourself be largely defined by just one role such as your job. (Montgomery 2002, 712)

How do you know when it's time to move on? If your salary is laughable, if you and your function are undervalued, if you suffer from a chronic and severe lack of support and resources, if your work environment is poisonous, get out. You owe it to yourself. Maybe you have just outgrown your job. Do you feel really comfortable, that you have all your tasks mastered? If you've tried developing a new service or taking on new responsibilities but still feel bored, take time to do a full analysis of your current situation and the future you want for yourself. "If the main goal is a high salary, one might want to look in the corporate sector. If the main objective is autonomy and flexibility, information brokerage might be the best field to enter. Finally, if job security is the most important factor, traditional libraries [with a strong union or an academic library where the librarians can gain life tenure] would be the best option" (Blessinger 2002).

Think about your ideal job: size of library, degree of responsibility, title, area of the country (or world), benefits, salary, type of customers, or area of librarianship (public, academic, school). Once you have created your "wish list," take the first step. If you need to go back to school, investigate where, when, how, how much. If you want to move to a different geographic location, subscribe to a local newspaper and read all about the area. E-mail librarians in the area and see how they feel about their jobs. If you're interested in a certain organization or community, use the Web to locate more information about it. Then look for that new job. Put out the word that you're looking. Ask friends if they know of or foresee openings. Polish your résumé and review interviewing techniques. Caution: once you've got the job, don't forget to focus on your whole career. Update your personal development plan and stay alert to opportunities that fit it. Don't be afraid to change as you and the library profession change. With a little effort you can be in charge of your career. Finally, do what you enjoy and enjoy what you do. Life's too short for anything else!

Perhaps you are just starting out in librarianship. Conventional wisdom says that you should begin to plan your career path as early as possible in your career. Make a plan, but don't get too attached to it. "You cannot now expect to stay in a job throughout a career, or assume that your employer will chart a course for you through the organization" (Pantry 1997, 172). Each job must be a learning experience; don't jump to another job until you've learned everything you can on the current one. "Make sure you leave smarter than you started" (Shontz 2002, 73). Your career plan should have continuing education built into it. Plan for nearly constant reevaluation, both of your skills and of the needs of employers. You will need to know about

   business and finance, to operate your library effectively;

   presentation skills, to be able to talk to groups with confidence;

   library technology, or at least the ability to use, teach, and write specifications for purchasing new technology;

   negotiating skills, both to obtain proper funding and support for programs and services and to ensure you are paid what you are worth; and

   sales and marketing skills, to meet the needs of current customers, attract new customers, and extend the library's reach beyond its immediate community.

## Giving Back: To Current and Future Colleagues

An important part of being a professional is the obligation to give back to the profession. You learned from and were helped by others and should do the same for those who follow. Write about your experiences. "Document and publish what your information center is doing . . . to people within our organizations or around the world . . . to help our colleagues learn from our experiences" (Sarmiento 2001, 6). Begin with newsletters put out by local chapters or subject divisions of your professional association. Then there are the specialty publications like *The One-Person Library, MLS: Marketing Library Services,* or *Searcher;* electronic newsletters like *Ex Libris: An E-Zine for Librarians and Other Information Junkies;* and large-format "newspapers" like *Information Today* or *Information World Review.* To reach a wider audience there are the library association journals like *American Libraries, Information Outlook, InCite* (Australia), or *Library + Information Update* (United Kingdom). Submit research articles to one of the more scholarly journals such as *Library Trends, The Australian Library Journal, Law Library*

*Journal, Aslib Proceedings,* or any of the Haworth Press journals (*Journal of Hospital Librarianship,* for instance). Like anything else, the more you write, the easier it gets—and the easier it gets to be published.

How do you think most leaders got to be leaders? Many began by volunteering in their professional associations. Here's one librarian's story. "From both LLSDC and AALL [Law Librarians' Society of Washington, D.C., and American Association of Law Libraries], I gained hands-on experience in the strategic planning process and language" (Ahearn 2002, 4). Carolyn P. Ahearn first volunteered to help ease her professional isolation and to meet and learn from her colleagues. She also learned to negotiate with vendors and developed confidence. You can start by serving on a committee, progress to chair, then to local or chapter office, and—before you know it—you are being asked by the national officers to serve on a national committee or even run for national office. I had never spoken formally in public before I became chair of the Solo Librarians Division of the Special Libraries Association, and I doubt if anyone outside of Cleveland had heard of me. I quickly learned not to be afraid of the microphone. My presentation and leadership skills improved with every meeting or speech. Now I confidently present workshops all over the world and am invited to speak at conferences. The confidence and skills you develop through volunteering will carry over to your work as well.

The third way you can give back is to help students. Volunteer to talk to a class or a student organization at your alma mater or a library school near you. Offer to serve as an advisor to a student chapter of one of the library associations. Speak at career days at high schools about librarianship as a career and help identify good prospective librarians and guide them toward a library career. Become a mentor to a student or new librarian. Offer a student internship or practicum experience. This does involve a lot of work, but you get free (or low-cost) assistance by an interested preprofessional, and a student receives invaluable on-the-job training.

## Improving the Image of the Profession

> "All librarians must engage in ongoing advocacy to guarantee the long-term survival and prosperity of their individual institutions and the library profession as a whole." (Kirchner 1999, 844)

More and more library schools are dropping the *L* word and substituting *information science* or just *information.* Many librarians and their employers are doing the same. Marylaine Block writes, "My own library was briefly called a Learning Resource Center. . . . It was supposed to indicate that the library now included media as well as stuffy old books and journals. But when anybody would tell students to go to the Learning Resource Center, they'd stare blankly until light would dawn and they'd say, 'Oh, the *library*.' It's far easier to make 'library' mean a place that includes media, too, than it is to make Learning Resource Center mean anything at all" (2000c). I experienced the same situation. I once had a boss who "hated" the word *library* and insisted I change the name of my facility. I did—to Corporate Information and Research Center (CIRC). I answered the telephone "Research Center." The response was invariably, "Is this the library?" I chose to become a librarian. I am a librarian. I am proud of being a librarian. Instead of taking the *L* word out of our job descriptions and schools, I would rather see the profession concentrate on changing the way people think of libraries and librarians. Finally, from a retired corporate librarian:

> You chose this profession. If it isn't right for you or if the job you're in is not a good match, get out! You can't expect that your management will always see things your way, that you will always have the budget you want, that your salary will always keep pace with your desires. Stop whining, consider what you can do about it, take steps, and move on. Having said all that I do have some concerns about the library profession. The trend I see is toward less professionalism. By that I mean that end-user services provided via Internet, outsourcing, etc. are making librarians more purchasing agents, contract administrators, and clerks. It's not that our patrons no longer need our help in finding information, but the day-to-day pressures of trying to provide and maintain the varied new tools make it very difficult to keep our own skills sharp. We must stay focused on providing information service. It's our job to help our clients refine their questions, to determine what sources are best used, to hone our understanding of search strategies and search systems, and to teach those users who want to do it themselves. That's where the professionalism resides and, to my way of thinking, that's where the fun is. (Appel 2002, 9)

Many people think that anyone who works in a library is a librarian—including clerks, pages, and other nonprofessionals. We can't even agree within the profession on the definition of a librarian. Some say that only graduates of accredited library schools are librarians. The degree does show a degree of commitment to the profession, but many experienced nonprofessionals are excellent librarians. The degree is only a starting point on the road to becoming a "real" librarian. Some non-professionals have already trod that road. My definition of a librarian is "a dedicated individual who works in a library—a library broadly defined as a place where answers are found for questions people have in their business and personal lives." A librarian is also someone who answers other people's questions as if they were his or her own. A librarian should be proud to be called a librarian and should constantly strive to improve the perception of a library and a librarian by the public and the profession.

There are additional problems of our own making. Allowing others (mostly computer people) to co-opt the word *information*. Complacency. The rise of weak library managers who were never trained in manage-ment. Relying on performance measures such as growth and use, instead of ones emphasizing the value we add.

## What Should Our Image Be?

If the images above aren't how we want others to see us, what image do we want? Some librarians want to be known as the information guru. Tom Peters states that "a guru is anyone who, anytime there's a ques-tion about [whatever], people say see Mary on the fourteenth floor" (Cyr 1998, 34). To be a guru you must specialize in one area, advertise what you know, and be willing to share your knowledge. That is indeed what good librarians do. But is it enough?

The U.S. Department of Transportation suggested that the role of the information professional is to "create, access, and evaluate sec-ondary information sources and provide quality, filtered information" based on customer requirements. "One area in which information pro-fessionals may be particularly valuable to users is in navigating the myriad new information products and services." Also valuable is assess-ing the value of information from online services and the Web. All of this is designed to "minimize the time spent looking for information" (Volpe 1998, 13). S. R. Ranganathan said that we must save the time of the user, but is this enough?

Ruth Holst and Sharon A. Phillips (2000) outlined the roles that health-care librarians play. These include service providers, business managers and administrators, technology managers (extending their expertise to other departments), patient educators, continuing medical education (CME) coordinators, and in-house educators and trainers. Other roles include serving on the institutional review boards, working on quality or performance improvement teams, and even managing other departments (such as audiovisual, archives, or medical records). Connie M. Schardt (1998) connects some of these roles directly to the Joint Commission on Accreditation of Healthcare Organizations (JCAHO) accreditation manual. JCAHO requires patients to be informed of other resources in the community. The library could provide information and referral services. Accreditation also requires hospitals to provide information to patients and families. The library could provide materials appropriate to age, culture, and reading level. JCAHO requires continuous improvement of patient health outcomes. The librarian could perform literature reviews to keep competitive intelligence teams current and to compare the hospital to others (benchmarking). Finally, accreditation requires showing leadership. The librarian could become involved with the leaders of the hospital and providing and tracking CE and study materials. This is better, but still is not enough.

Many librarians have taken jobs with new titles, new opportunities, and higher salaries. They are now LAN administrators, Webmasters, knowledge managers, systems librarians, and chief information officers (CIOs) (Blessinger 2002). Is this good for the profession? I doubt it. If anything, it demeans it because it sends the message that you have to leave the job of "librarian" behind to be powerful in an organization. Just a title or job change is definitely not enough. "Librarians in CIO roles offer the ability to examine the nature of information, assess what information is needed and used by the organization, and discover why the information is needed" (Greer 1998, 90). Anthea Stratigos observed that "CIOs really don't know about managing content. So the information professionals are seeing their roles broadening to overall collection management and overall content deployment" and suggests that organizations should have two positions: CTO (chief technology officer)—a computer expert—and a CIO (chief information officer)—a librarian (Pemberton 1999, 46). This would go a long way toward improving the image of the profession, but it is still not enough.

Thomas Davenport and Laurence Prusak, in their "Rules for Tomorrow's Informational Professional," take us a bit farther down the right road.

1. Get out of the library and into the business.
2. Actively assess who needs information and who has it—then help them to connect.
3. Focus on multiple media and how they can be exploited using tomorrow's technologies.
4. Develop an alliance with the more user-oriented IS [Information Services] personnel.

5. Don't assume that technology will replace humans in information provision.
6. Develop an architecture of information.
7. Work with external providers to develop more useful vehicles for information.
8. Emphasize usage of information materials over control (n.d., 9, Exhibit 2).

Stephen Abram (2000) adds, "Our goal is not wisdom, but to positively impact *behaviour* in our enterprises and society." And Bruce W. Dearstyne states that "information professionals need to help people formulate and articulate their information needs and to work toward empowering them to meet those needs on their own rather than (or in addition to) relying on the information professional as an intermediary" (2000, 34–36). Now we're getting really close.

I think the following best describes the mind-set we need to adopt. "Our world demands for us, the information professionals of the twenty-first century, to think and behave like CEOs, and our information centers to be like corporations. We must strive to be creative and dynamic, either by generating our own ideas or by 'borrowing' them from successful organizations and applying them to our own settings" (Sarmiento 2001, 7). "The information manager's mission should be to serve as the primary conduit for transmission of information from wherever it exists to wherever it is needed" (Shamel 2002, 65). We need to move beyond the old model of being the person others come to for information. We need to become the person who reaches out to others to bring them the answers—or perhaps the means to discover those answers for themselves. That is the librarian model for the twenty-first century.

Now that we know where we're going, how are we going to get there? What can we, should we, must we do to change the image of the profession of librarianship? Block had some ideas: "It's past time that we explained the value we're giving for money, not in the mind-numbing prose of annual reports nobody's ever going to read, but in simple, understandable bullet points. It's also time for us to explain what librarians do . . . on our web sites, on bookmarks, in newsletters, [and] in reports to the people who make funding decisions." Block created a list, "What We Do with Your Tax Dollars," stating where the dollars are spent:

X dollars to license X number of databases that provide online access from home or office to articles in thousands of magazines, newspapers, and reference books.

X dollars to maintain the library web site, where people can search our catalog and databases as well as our recommended web sites.

X dollars to pay the friendly support staff who smile and chat while they check out your materials to you.

X dollars for professional librarians who this year have

answered X number of questions, by phone, e-mail, chat, and in person

selected and cataloged the best books to meet your needs

selected X number of outstanding web resources . . .

read X number of books out loud to X number of kids during story hours . . .

provided homework help to X number of students

installed X number of software packages, troubleshot X number of computer and printer crashes, and kept X number of workstations open and accessible to our users

taken X number of classes and workshops to learn new technologies and search tools

written and distributed X number of reading lists and instructions for using databases, CD-ROMs, e-books, the internet, and other technologies. (Block 2002)

It is impossible to discuss improving the image of librarianship as a profession without someone bringing up the issue of low pay. The cruel truth is that, for the most part, we librarians are not paid what we think we are worth. As long as we accept the salaries that are being paid, there is no reason for employers to raise our pay. We knew (or should have known) the pay situation when we went into this profession. Yes, we should be paid more, but we live in a capitalist economy, and, as a rule, capitalism does not pay people to do what they enjoy. (Yes, doctors get paid to do what they enjoy, but there is a big difference in years of schooling, level of stress and responsibility, and costs of doing business between librarianship and medicine.) I often ask librarians if there is any other job they'd prefer to be doing, and almost always the answer is no. We might keep professional positions open if a professional can't be hired at the available salary, or we could boycott low-paying positions, but I doubt either approach would work. There will always be someone who really needs that position and will take the job anyway. In March 2002 the New South Wales (NSW) Industrial Relations Commission in Australia recognized that librarians, library assistants, and library technicians in NSW public service, state libraries, government agencies, and universities "have been historically undervalued despite very significant increases in their skills and output over the past decade"; said that they were professionals "on equal footing with lawyers [and] engineers"; and granted them one-time pay raises of up to 26 percent (Teece 2002, 8). There is a fear that rising salaries will force some public libraries to close because of too-high payrolls. It will be interesting to see how this develops.

In conclusion, if we make ourselves the information experts, keep our eyes open for opportunities, learn how to make our own breaks, and are prepared to work hard, we can be an important part of the information future. Users may take the technology for granted, but they will always need the services we can provide—assuming that we let them know what we can do. Robert F. Muir wrote, "A physicist may take eight years to formulate, and a biochemist one day to replicate, but a librarian can do ten years of research in an hour—that's powerful! But does anyone out there *know*?" (1993, 41). That's the problem in a nutshell. *We* know what we can do, but everyone else does not. We have been invisible far too long. It is time to take off our cloak of invisibility, timidity, complacency, and modesty and reveal ourselves to the world as we really are and can be—The *Visible* Librarian!

# SOURCES CITED

Abram, Stephen. 1996. Market your valuable experience. *MLS: Marketing Library Services* (Oct./Nov.): 87–88.

———. 2000. Shift happens: Ten key trends in our profession and ten strategies for success. *The Serials Librarian* 38(1/2): 41–59; copublished simultaneously in Fiander, P. Michelle, Joseph C. Harmon, and Jonathan David Makepeace. 2000. *From Carnegie to Internet2: Forging the serials future.* Binghamton, N.Y.: Haworth, 41–59.

———. 2002. Marketing searchers in the shifting sands of search. *Information Outlook* 6(11): 44–45.

Adams, Kate E., and Mary Cassner. 2001. Marketing library resources and services to distance faculty. *Journal of Library Administration* 31(3/4): 5–22.

Adams, Wendi. 2002. In SOLOLIB-L [electronic list], July 9.

Ahearn, Carolyn P. 2002. Volunteering: The origin of the species. *PLL Perspectives* 13(3): 1, 4.

Apelt, Brian. 2001. Avoid these eight common marketing mistakes. *COSE Update* 24(10): 17–19.

Appel, Linda. 2002. I was a solo librarian: A career retrospective. *The One-Person Library: A Newsletter for Librarians and Management* 18(11): 8–9.

Bacon, Mark S. 1992. *Do it yourself direct marking: Secrets for small business.* New York: Wiley.
    Many examples of direct mail pieces.

Baker, Lynda M., and Virginia Manbeck. 2002. *Consumer health information for public librarians.* Lanham, Md.: Scarecrow.

    Especially chapter 6, "Promoting the CHI Collection and Service."

Baldwin, Jerry. 2002. The crisis in special libraries: An overview and case study. *Sci-Tech News* 56(2): 4–11.

Banker, Laurey. 2002. More than a sound bite . . . sound publicity strategies. Presentation to the Heights Regional Chamber of Commerce,
June 27, Cleveland Heights, Ohio.

Bardwick, J. M. 1986. *The plateauing trap: How to avoid it in your career . . .
and your life.* New York: American Management Assn.

Barter, Richard F., Jr. 1994. In search of excellence in libraries: The management writing of Tom Peters and their implications for library and
information services. *Library Management* 15(8): 4–15.

Beckwith, Harry. 1997. *Selling the invisible: A field guide to modern marketing.* New York: Warner.

> An absolute must-read for every librarian. The "invisible" is service!

———. 2000. *The invisible touch: The four keys to modern marketing.* New
York: Warner.

> If you can't locate *Selling the Invisible,* this is a good substitute.

Bell, Chip R. 1994. *Customers as partners: Building relationships that last.*
San Francisco: Berrett-Koehler.

> One of the best customer service books I've read.

Bell, Hope. 1998. Blowing your own horn. *Information Highways* 5(4): 7.

Berry, Tim, and Doug Wilson. 2001. *On target: The book on marketing
plans.* 2d ed. Eugene, Oreg.: Palo Alto Software. Supplied with
Marketing Plan Pro software.

Besant, Larry X., and Deborah Sharp. 2000. Upsize this! Libraries need
relationship marketing. *Information Outlook* 4(3): 17–22.

Blessinger, Kelly. 2002. Trends in the job market for librarians:
1985–2000. *Electronic Journal of Academic and Special Librarianship*
3(1). Available at <http://www.southernlibrarianship.icaap.org/
content/v03n01/Blessinger_k01.htm>.

Block, Marylaine. 2000a. Community outreach as a survival strategy. *Ex
Libris: An E-Zine for Librarians and Other Information Junkies* (80).
Available at <http://www.marylaine.com/exlibris/>.

———. 2000b. Training our bosses. *Ex Libris: An E-Zine for Librarians and
Other Information Junkies* (46). Available at <http://www.marylaine.
com/exlibris/>.

———. 2000c. Librarian and library: Perfectly good words. *Ex Libris: An
E-Zine for Librarians and Other Information Junkies* (49). Available at
<http://www.marylaine.com/exlibris/>.

———. 2002. A predictable funding disaster. *Ex Libris: An E-Zine for
Librarians and Other Information Junkies* (149). Available at <http://
www.marylaine.com/exlibris/>.

Brown, Suzan A. 1997. Marketing the corporate information center for success. *Online* (July/Aug.): 74–79.

Bryant, Sue Lacey. 1995. *Personal professional development and the solo librarian.* London: Library Assn.

Buchanan, Holly Shipp. 2000. Human resources management. In *The Medical Library Association guide to managing health care libraries,* edited by Ruth Holst and Sharon A. Phillips. New York: Neal-Schuman.

Casey, James B. 2002. The 1.6% solution. *American Libraries* 33(4): 85–86.

Cavill, Patricia. 2001. Advocacy: How does it differ from public relations and marketing? *Feliciter* 47(2): 90-93.

Chochrek, Denise. 2000. Market the value of your competitive intelligence: An added role for the information center. *Information Outlook* 4(2): 32–35.

Coote, Helen, and Bridget Batchelor. 1997. *How to market your library service effectively.* 2d ed. London: Aslib.

Corcoran, Mary. 2002. How to survive and thrive in the new economy: Follow the money. *Online* 26(3): 76–77.

Cram, Jennifer. 1995. Moving from cost centre to profitable investment: Managing the perception of a library's worth. *Aplis* 8(3): 107–13.

Curci-Gonzalez, Luci. 2000. All I really need to know about law library marketing I learned watching commercials during the Super Bowl. *AALL Spectrum* 4(6): 16.

Cyr, Diane. 1998. Genius at work: The guru game (an interview with Tom Peters). *Attaché* (Sept.): 34–37.

Davenport, Thomas, and Laurence Prusak. n.d. Blow up the corporate library. *Ernst & Young Research Note.* Ernst & Young.

Dearstyne, Bruce W. 2000. Greeting and shaping the future: Information professionals as strategists and leaders. *Information Outlook* 4(8): 32–36.

Deitch, Joseph. 1984. Portrait: Marvin Scilken. *Wilson Library Bulletin* 59(3): 205-7.

———. 2002. A conversation with Marvin H. Scilken. In *Getting libraries the credit they deserve: A Festschrift in honor of Marvin H. Scilken,* edited by Loriene Roy and Antony Cherian. Lanham, Md.: Scarecrow.

Dempsey, Kathy. 2002. Visibility: Decloaking "the invisible librarian." *Searcher* 10(7): 76–81.

Dimick, Barbara. 1995. Marketing youth services. *Library Trends* 43(3): 463–77.

Dobson, Chris. 2002. Beyond the information audit: Checking the health of an organization's information system. *Searcher* 10(7): 32–37.

Drucker, Peter. 1985. *Innovation and entrepreneurship.* New York: Harper and Row.

Dworkin, Kristine D. 2001. Library marketing: Eight ways to get unconventionally creative. *Online* 25(1): 52–54.

Ebbinghouse, Carol. 2002a. Library outsourcing: A new look. *Searcher* 10(4): 63–68.

———. 2002b. Would you hire you? Continuing education for the information professional. *Searcher* 10(7): 110–15.

Eckholt, Larry E. 2001. Using a character for library publicity. *MLS: Marketing Library Services* 14(1). Available at <http://www.infotoday. com/mls/jan00/howto.htm>.

Ellis, Anne V. 1999. Managing the management: The firm and the private law. *Legal Reference Services Quarterly* 17(3): 27–31.

Evans, G. Edward, Patricia Layzell Ward, and Bendik Ruggas. 2000. *Management basics for information professionals.* New York: Neal-Schuman.

  If you only get one book, this should be it. Very comprehensive. Updated at <http://www.neal-schuman.com/managementbasics. htmla> or <http://www.lmu.edu/mbiF>.

Flood, Marilyn J. 1999. Librarian and management in partnership. In *Managing the law library 1999: Forging effective relationships in today's law office,* edited by Karin V. Donahue et al. Intellectual Property Course Handbook Series, no. G-546. New York: Practising Law Institute.

Forbes, Linda. 1998. De-privatised librarian: Interview with Chris Richardson. Available at <http://www.its.utas.edu.au/info/march98/ chrisr.html>.

Fosmire, Michael. 2001. Bibliographic instruction in physics libraries: A survey of current practice and tips for marketing BI. *Science and Technology Libraries* 19(2): 25–34.

Gallacher, Cathryn. 1999. *Managing change in libraries and information services.* London: Aslib.

Garcia, Jenny Leigh. 2000. Dispelling the myths: Quantifying what librarians really do. *Business Information Alert* 12(6): 1–3, 6.

Gaynor, Kathy M. 2002. In LIBREF-L [electronic list], August 7.

Graham, Laurel. 2002. In MEDLIB-L [electronic list], July 9.

Greer, Marsha C. 1998. The medical librarian as chief information officer. *Bulletin of the Medical Library Association* 86(1): 88–94.

Griffiths, José-Marie, and Donald W. King. 1993. *Special libraries: Increasing the information edge.* Washington, D.C.: Special Libraries Assn.

Gupta, Dinesh K., and Ashok Jambhekar. 2002. Which way do you want to serve your customers? *Information Outlook* 6(7): 26–31.

Hadden, F. Lee. 2002. Dress for other reasons. Available on LIBREF-L, June 13.

Hamilton, Feona. 1990. *Infopromotion: Publicity and marketing ideas for the information profession.* Aldershot, U.K.: Gower.

Good for specifics on public relations vehicles but has only British examples.

Hammond, Patricia A., and Margy Priddy. 2001. Hospital libraries are an economically sound investment. *MLA News* (341): 1, 10.

Hane, Paula J. 2002. Report from the field: InfoToday 2002. *Information Today* 19(7): 1, 35.

Henczel, Susan. 2001. *The information audit: A practical guide.* Munich: Saur.

Hernon, Peter, and Ellen Altman. 1998. *Assessing service quality: Satisfying the expectations of library customers.* Chicago: American Library Assn.

Focuses on public and academic libraries.

Hernon, Peter, and John R. Whitman. 2001. *Delivering satisfaction and service quality: A customer-based approach for libraries.* Chicago: American Library Assn.

Good examples of mission statements and goals. Public and academic library focus.

Hiam, Alexander. 2000. *Marketing kit for dummies.* Foster City, Calif.: IDG Books.

Comes with a CD-ROM with design and marketing templates, lists, and examples.

Hoey, Peter. 1999. Marketing the Library and Information Centre of the Royal Society of Chemistry. *Managing Information* 6(7): 47–49.

Holst, Ruth, and Sharon A. Phillips, eds. 2000. *The Medical Library Association guide to managing health care libraries.* New York: Neal-Schuman.

Excellent!

Hu, Robert H. 2002. PR for academic libraries: Focus on the faculty. *AALL Spectrum* 6(5): 28, 32.

Hubbard, Marlis. 2002. Exploring the sabbatical or other leave as a means of energizing a career. *Library Trends* 50(4): 603–13.

Hurst, Jill Ann. 2001a. A different view: A tenor and a marketer. *The One-Person Library: A Newsletter for Librarians and Management* 18(2): 6–7.

————.2001b. A tourist in the library. *The One-Person Library: A Newsletter for Librarians and Management* 18(3): 14–15.

————. 2001c. Presenting marketing information. *The One-Person Library: A Newsletter for Librarians and Management* 18(6): 8–9.

————. 2002. Staying on top of your game: A learning strategy. *Searcher* 10(7): 72–75.

Infield, Neil. 2002. Our customers are people—not "end users." *Information World Review* (180): 12.

Jacobs, Leslie, and Mary Corcoran. 2002. Lessons from library closings. *Information Briefing* 5(9): 1–9.

Jain, Abhinandan K., Ashok Jambhekar, T. P. Rama Rao, and S. Sreenivas Rao, eds. 1999. *Marketing information products and services: A primer for librarians and information professionals.* Ottawa, Canada: International Development Research Centre.

Kamm, Sue. 2002. A modest proposal. In NEWLIB-L [electronic list], April 1.

Karp, Rashelle. 1995. *Part-time public relations with full-time results: A PR primer for libraries.* Chicago: American Library Assn. Written for the Public Relations Section of the Library Administration and Management Association.

Kassel, Amelia. 2002. Practical tips to help you prove your value. *MLS: Marketing Library Services* 16(4): 1–4.

Kendall, Sandra, and Susan Massarella. 2001. Prescription for successful marketing. *Computers in Libraries* 21(8): 28–32.

Kennedy, Mary Lee. 1996. Positioning strategic information: Partnering for the information advantage. *Special Libraries* 87(2): 120–31.

Kirchner, Terry. 1999. Advocacy 101 for academic librarians: Tips to help your institution prosper. *College and Research Libraries News* (Nov.): 844–49.

Koch, Richard. 1998. *The 80/20 principle: The secret of achieving more with less.* New York: Doubleday.

Koontz, Christine M. 2002. Stores and libraries: Both serve customers. *MLS: Marketing Library Services* 16(1): 3–6.

La Rosa, Sharon M. 1992. Marketing slays the downsizing dragon. *Information Today* 9(3): 58–59.

Interview with Betty Edwards.

Lavoie, Lisa. 2002. Throwing a party to meet all of our patrons' needs. *MLS: Marketing Library Services* 16(5): 1–3.

Leerburger, Benedict A. 1989. *Promoting and marketing the library.* Rev. ed. Boston: Hall. Out of print.

Lemon, Nancy. 1996. Climbing the value chain: A case study in rethinking the corporate library function. *Online* (Nov.). Available at <http://www.infotoday.com/online/NovOL/lemon11.html>.

Levinson, Jay Conrad. 1998. *Guerilla marketing: Secrets for making big profits from your small business.* 3d ed. Boston: Houghton Mifflin.

Line, Maurice B. 2002. Management musings eight: To see ourselves as users see us . . . *Library Management* 23(6/7): 338–39.

Lower, William E. 1921. What is a patient? Sign posted at the admitting desk at the Cleveland Clinic.

Lum, Moya. 2000. Flexibility and responsiveness: The key to success. *InCite* 21(4): 12.

Mackay, Harvey. 1997. *Dig your well before you're thirsty: The only networking book you'll ever need.* New York: Currency/Doubleday.

> Fantastic! The subtitle is really true.

MacLeod, Roddy, and Lesa Ng. n.d. Shoestring marketing: Examples from EEVL. *Ariadne* (27). Available at <http://www.ariadne.ac.uk/issue27/eevl>.

> EEVL is a portal for engineering, mathematics, and computing from the Heriot-Watt University library in Edinburgh.

Marshall, Cathy. 2002. Interview by author, Richmond Heights, Ohio, July 9.

Maslow, A. H. 1943. A theory of human motivation. *Psychological Review* 50: 394–95.

Matarazzo, James M., and Laurence Prusak. 1997. *The value of corporate libraries: Findings from a 1995 survey of senior management.* Washington, D.C.: Special Libraries Assn. Out of print.

McCarthy, Grace. 1992. Promoting the in-house library. *Aslib Proceedings* 44(7/8): 289–93.

> Four case studies.

McClellan, Susan Peterman. 2001. Solo librarians and socialization. *The One-Person Library: A Newsletter for Librarians and Management* 17(10): 8–9.

McKenna, Regis. 1997. *Real time: Preparing for the age of the never satisfied customer.* Boston: Harvard Business School Pr.

McKinnon, Sharon M., and William J. Bruns Jr. 1992. *The information mosaic: How managers get the information they really need.* Boston: Harvard Business School Pr.

> Deals only with accounting information.

McLaughlin-Shuereb, Donna. 1998. Bulletin board workshop, Annual Conference of the Church and Synagogue Library Association, Cleveland, Ohio.

McMillen, Paula. 2001. Practice makes perfect (or, at least better!) *Info Career Trends* 2(5). Available at <http://www.lisjobs.com>.

Mieszkowski, Katharine. 1999. Digital competition—Avram Miller. *Fast Company* (30): 156. Available at <http://www.fastcompany.com/online/30/miller.html#>.

Montgomery, Denise L. 2002. Happily ever after: Plateauing as a means for long-term career satisfaction. *Library Trends* 50(4): 702–16.

Muir, Robert F. 1993. Marketing your library or information service to business. *Online* (July): 41–46.

   He is *not* a librarian but an expert in business-to-business marketing, licensing, and commercialization of technology.

Newell, Frederick. 1997. *The new rules of marketing: How to use one-to-one relationship marketing to be the leader in your industry.* New York: McGraw-Hill.

Nicholas, David. 2000. *Assessing information needs: Tools, techniques and concepts for the Internet age.* 2d ed. London: Aslib.

Oder, Norman. 2002. State library agency and collection in Minnesota gutted, state PL funding slashed in AR, CO. *Library Journal* 127(12): 14–15.

Olson, Christine. 2002. Grooming passionate library evangelists: Communicating the value of information services. Special Libraries Association Virtual Seminar, April 24.

Pace, Andrew K. 2000. Marketing our strengths. *Computers in Libraries* (Sept.): 63–65.

Pantry, Sheila. 1997. Whither the information profession? Challenges and opportunities: The cultivation of information professionals for the new millennium. *Aslib Proceedings* 49(6): 170–72.

Pemberton, Jeff. 1999. An industry analysis with Outsell, Inc. *Online* (July/Aug.): 40–46.

   An interview with Anthea Stratigos of Outsell, Inc.

Peppers, Don, and Martha Rogers. 1997. *Enterprise one to one: Tools for competing in the interactive age.* New York: Currency/Doubleday.

Phillips, Sharon A. 1990. Productivity measurement in hospital libraries: A case report. *Bulletin of the Medical Library Association* 78(2): 146–53.

Ranganathan, S. R. 1964. *The five laws of library science.* Bombay, N.Y.: Asia Pub. House.

Rashid, Shahida, and Taodhg Burns. 1998. Innovation and survival: A case study in planning medical library services. *Bulletin of the Medical Library Association* 86(4): 508–17.

Reed, Sally Gardner. 2001. *Making the case for your library.* How-to-Do-It-Manual, no. 104. New York: Neal-Schuman.

Many good examples of good PR, sample letters.

Reuben, L., and A. Carter. 2001. Customer service: Pitfalls and potentialities. Ninth Specials, Health and Law Libraries Conference, Australian Library and Information Association. Available at <http://www.alia.org.au/conferences/shllc/2001/papers/reuben.carter.html>.

Ries, Al. 1996. *Focus: The future of your company depends on it.* New York: HarperBusiness.

Many examples with pearls of wisdom sprinkled in.

Ries, Al, and Jack Trout. 1981. *Positioning: The battle for your mind: How to be seen and heard in the overcrowded marketplace.* New York: Warner.

A classic.

Robinson, Regan. 2002. Selection with Scilken. In *Getting libraries the credit they deserve: A Festschrift in honor of Marvin H. Scilken,* edited by Loriene Roy and Antony Cherian. Lanham, Md.: Scarecrow.

Rosen, Nathan A. 1999. Continuing education: The ever-evolving role of librarians. In *Managing the law library 1999: Forging effective relationships in today's law office,* edited by Karin V. Donahue et al. Intellectual Property Course Handbook Series, no. G-546. New York: Practising Law Institute.

Sarmiento, Roberto A. 2001. A call to action. *Sci-Tech News* (Nov.): 6–10. A publication of the Science-Technology Division, Special Libraries Association.

Sass, Rivkah K. 2002. Marketing the worth of your library. *Library Journal* 127(11): 37–38.

Sawyer, Deborah C. 2002. *Smart services: Competitive information strategies, solutions and success stories for service businesses.* Medford, N.J.: Information Today.

Schardt, Connie M. 1998. Going beyond information management: Using the *Comprehensive accreditation manual for hospitals* to promote knowledge-based information services. *Bulletin of the Medical Library Association* 86(4): 504–7.

Schneiderman, R. Anders. 1997. A non-librarian explains "why librarians should rule the Net." *Information Outlook* 1(4): 34–35.

Scilken, Marvin. 1979. Let's put some realism in public library public relations. *Unabashed Librarian* (30): 11.

———. 1982. Editor's mumblings. *Unabashed Librarian* (42): 2.

———. 1994. Editor's note. *Unabashed Librarian* (93): 10.

Seacord, Stephanie. 1999. *Public relations marketing: Making a splash without much cash.* Central Point, Oreg.: Oasis Pr.

Seddon, Sandra. 1990. Marketing library and information services. *Library Management* 11(6): 35–39.

> Has an excellent bibliography.

Shamel, Cynthia. 2002. Building a brand: Got librarian? *Searcher* 10(7): 60–71.

Shear, Joan. 2001. Are you PR impaired? How would you know? *AALL Spectrum* 5(5): 14, 17, 30.

Shimpock-Vieweg, Kathy. 1992. How to develop a marketing plan for a law firm library. *Law Library Journal* 84: 67–91.

> Has an excellent sample marketing plan.

Shisler, Carol M. 2000. Positive image and high profile gets results in a hospital library. *Bulletin of the Medical Library Association* 88(3): 251–53.

Shontz, Priscilla K. 2002. *Jump start your career in library and information science.* Lanham, Md.: Scarecrow.

> Includes skills lists, descriptions of a day in the life of various types of librarians.

Shucha, Bonnie. 2002. Tips for marketing a law library web site. *AALL Spectrum* 6(6): 12–13, 21.

Shuck, Jay. 2002. It looks like rain. *Law Libraries in the New Millennium* 4(3): 4–5.

> Profile of Terri Lawrence, law librarian.

Sirkin, Arlene Farber. 1991. Marketing planning for maximum effectiveness. *Special Libraries* 82(winter): 1–6.

Slocum, Charlotte. 2002. Letter to author, July 15.

Smith, Sally Decker. 2002. Sally in Libraryland. *The Illinois Library Association Reporter* 20(3): 14–15.

Soules, Aline. 2001. The principles of marketing and relationship management. *Portal: Libraries and the Academy* 1(3): 339–50.

St. Clair, Guy. 1993. *Customer service in the information environment.* Information Services Management Series. London: Bowker-Saur.

———. 1994. *Power and influence: Enhancing information services within the organization.* Information Services Management Series. London: Bowker-Saur.

St. Clair, Guy, and Joan Williamson. 1992. *Managing the new one-person library*. London: Bowker-Saur.

> Especially relevant: chapter 4, "Training and Continuing Education"; chapter 7, "Advocacy"; chapter 13, "Marketing."

Stear, Edward B. 1997. The successful manager: Ten ways to gain management support for key projects (or, all I need to know to manipulate management I learned as a teenager). *Online* (May). Available at <http://www.infotoday.com/online/May97/manager5.html>.

Strouse, Roger. 2002. Thriving in an uncertain environment. *CILIP Library + Information Update* 1(4): 48–49.

Swart, Sarah Legarde. 2000. Marketing my corporate library on the Web. *MLS: Marketing Library Services* 14(7). Available at <http://www. infotoday.com/MLS: Marketing Library Services/oct00/.swart.htm>.

Talley, Mary, and Joan Axelroth. 2001. Talking about customer service. *Information Outlook* 5(12): 6–13.

Teece, Phil. 2002. Hard slog wins best-ever wage decision. *InCite* 23(5): 8–9.

Tennant, Roy. 2001. The convenience catastrophe. *Library Journal* 126(20): 39–40.

Tolman, Jay W. 1998. *Marketing for the new millennium: Applying new techniques*. Central Point, Oreg.: Oasis Pr.

Tomlin, Anne C. 1999. Looking for that nudge. *The One-Person Library: A Newsletter for Librarians and Management* 16(5): 10–11.

Tovell, Chris. 2001. Whippersnappers vs. the old guard? Making e-resources training a collaborative experience. *Info Career Trends* 2(5). Available at <http://www.lisjobs.com>.

Trout, Jack, with Steve Rivkin. 1996. *The new positioning: The latest on the world's #1 business strategy*. New York: McGraw-Hill.

Usherwood, Bob. 1981. *The visible library: Practical public relations for public librarians*. London: Library Assn.

> Dated, but good. From the viewpoint of British public libraries.

———. 1991. The visible library in the 1990s. *Assistant Librarian* 84(12): 182–88.

———. 2002. Let's be professional. *Library Association Record* 104(2): 98–99.

Van Riel, Rachel. 2002. Getting past "G." *CILIP Library + Information Update* 1(5): 38–39.

Volpe National Transportation Systems Center, U.S. Department of Transportation. 1998. *Value of information and information services.* FHWA-SA-99-038. Washington, D.C.: U.S. Department of Transportation, Federal Highway Administration.

Wagner, Mary Lynn. 1997. Librarians, get out from behind your desks! *AALL Spectrum* 1(7): 32.

Weaver, Eris. 2002. In MEDLIB-L [electronic list], July 11.

Weiner, Barbara. n.d. "Marketing: Making a case for your library." Available at <http://www.nnlm.gov/gmr/3sources/0010.html>.

Weingand, Darlene E. 1994. *Managing today's public library: Blueprint for change.* Englewood, Colo.: Libraries Unlimited.

———. 1995. Marketing of library and information services. *Library Trends* 43(3): 289–513.

———. 1998. *Future-driven library marketing.* Chicago: American Library Assn.

Westbrook, Lynn. 2001. *Identifying and analyzing user needs: A complete handbook and ready-to-use assessment workbook with disk.* New York: Neal-Schuman.

> Oriented to public libraries but excellent ideas for all. Very thorough. Examples of academic, public, and school library user-needs study reports.

White, Herbert S. 1984. *Managing the special library: Strategies for success within the larger organization.* White Plains, N.Y.: Knowledge Industry.

———. 1996a. Our strategy for saving libraries: Add water to the thin soup. *Library Journal* 121(3): 126–27.

———. 1996b. The politics of reinventing special libraries. *Special Libraries* 82(winter): 59–62.

———. 1997. Marketing as a tool for destabilization. *Library Journal* 122(3): 116–17.

Williamson, Joan. 1996. Connecting the organizational mission and the library mission. *The One-Person Library: A Newsletter for Librarians and Management* 12(9): 3.

Wilson, Jerry R. 1991. *Word-of-mouth marketing.* New York: Wiley.

> With specific examples. Note "100 Little Things That Light Fires."

# ADDITIONAL RESOURCES

## INTRODUCTION

### WEBSITES

Glossary of Marketing Definitions:
<http://www.ifla.org/VII/s34/ pubs/glossary.htm>

Marketing Terms.com: <http://www.marketingterms.com/>

Target Marketing—direct marketing glossary:
<http://www.targetonline.com/sics/directmail.bsp>

## CHAPTER 1. THE PRIMACY OF CUSTOMER SERVICE AND OTHER BASICS

### BOOKS

Brinkman, Rick, and Rick Kirschner. 1994. *Dealing with people you can't stand: How to bring out the best in people at their worst.* New York: McGraw-Hill.

> Their "10 Most Unwanted List."

Roy, Loriene, and Antony Cherian, eds. 2002. *Getting libraries the credit they deserve: A Festschrift in honor of Marvin H. Scilken.* Lanham, Md.: Scarecrow, pp. 13–21.

St. Clair, Guy. 1997. *Customer service excellence: A concise guide for librarians.* Chicago: American Library Assn.

> Excellent. Many checklists and case studies.

Walters, Suzanne. 1994. *Customer service: A how-to-do-it-manual for librarians.* New York: Neal-Schuman.

## ARTICLES

Dinerman, Gloria. 2002. If you don't know, ask: The art and craft of surveys. *Information Outlook* 6(7): 6–10.

Evangelista, Ernie. 2001. Surviving change: A case study in marketing library services. *Business Information Alert* 13(7): 1, 3, 5, 9.

Leonicio, Maggie. 2001. Going the extra mile: Customer service with a smile. *The Reference Librarian* (72): 51–63.

Montanelli, Dale S., and Patricia F. Stenstrom, eds. 1999. *People come first: User-centered academic library service.* ACRL Publications in Librarianship, no. 53. Chicago: Association of College and Research Libraries.

Pedley, Paul. 2002. Coping with change. *Managing Information* 9(2): 18–19.

Stalker, John C. 1999. Reference: Putting users first. In *People come first: User-centered academic library service,* edited by Dale S. Montanelli and Patricia F. Stenstrom. ACRL Publications in Librarianship, no. 53. Chicago: Association of College and Research Libraries.

Thorpe, Suzanne. 2002. Trends in law library public services: Have you seen your patrons lately? *AALL Spectrum* 6(5): 6–7, 30.

# CHAPTER 2. DOING THE GROUND WORK: MARKETING

## BOOKS AND PERIODICALS

*Just about library retail.* Quarterly free electronic newsletter, John Stanley Associates, 142 Hummerston Road, Kalamunda, Western Australia, 6076, Australia; voice: 61-8-9293-4533, fax: 61-8-9293-4561, e-mail: info@johnstanley.cc, website: <http://www.johnstanley.cc>.

Kassel, Amelia. 2002. Practical tips to help you prove your value. *MLS: Marketing Library Services* 16(4): 1–4.

Kotler, Philip, and Alan Andreasen. 1996. *Strategic marketing for nonprofit organizations.* 5th ed. New York: Prentice-Hall.

Lancaster, F. W. 1988. *If you want to evaluate your library . . .* London: Library Associates.

McLeish, Barry J. 1995. *Successful marketing strategies for nonprofit organizations.* New York: Wiley.

*MLS: Marketing library services.* Published eight times a year by Information Today, Inc., and edited by Kathy Miller, Information Today, Inc., 143 Old Marlton Pike, Medford, NJ 08055-8750; voice:

1-609-654-6266 or 1-800-300-9868, fax: 1-609-654-4309, e-mail: kmiller@infotoday.com.

Highly recommended.

Portugal, Frank H. 2000. *Valuating information intangibles: Measuring the bottom line contribution of librarians and information professionals.* Washington, D.C.: Special Libraries Assn.

Ries, Al, and Jack Trout. 1994. *The twenty-two immutable laws of marketing: Violate them at your own risk.* New York: Harper Business.

Stanley, John. 1999. *Just about everything a retail manager needs to know.* John Stanley Associates, 142 Hummerston Road, Kalamunda, Western Australia, 6076, Australia; voice: 61-8-9293-4533, fax: 61-8-9293-4561, e-mail: info@johnstanley.cc, website: <http://www.johnstanley.cc>.

Trout, Jack, with Steve Rivkin. 1996. *The new positioning: The latest on the world's #1 business strategy.* New York: McGraw-Hill.

Urquhart, Christine J., and John B. Hepworth. 1995. *The value of information services to clinicians: A toolkit for measurement.* Aberystwyth, Wales: Department of Information and Library Studies, University of Wales, Aberystwyth, and the British Library Research and Development Department.

An excellent guide to doing a detailed customer needs analysis.

## ARTICLES

Abram, Stephen. 1996. Market your valuable experience. *MLS: Marketing Library Services* (Oct./Nov.): 87–88.

Ash, Joan S., and Elizabeth H. Wood. 2000. Marketing library services. In *Administration and management in health science libraries*, edited by Rick B. Forsman. Current Practices in Health Sciences Librarianship, vol. 8. Lanham, Md.: Scarecrow.

Ashcroft, Linda, and Clive Hoey. 2001. PR, marketing, and the Internet: Implications for information professionals. *Library Management* 22(1/2): 68–74.

Basch, Reva. 1997. Proactive marketing: Helping technologies emerge. *Searcher* 5(4): 50–51.

Bashe, Gil, and Nancy Hicks. 2001. Branding health services: Defining yourself in the marketplace. *Marketing Health Services* 21(1): 42–43.

Bridges, Peggy Bess, and Suzette Morgan. 2000. Creatively marketing the corporate library. *MLS: Marketing Library Services* 14(2). Available at <http://www.infotoday.com/mls/mar00/bridges&morgan.htm>.

Bunyan, Linda E., and Evelyn M. Lutz. 1991. Marketing the hospital library to nurses. *Bulletin of the Medical Library Association* 79(2): 223–25.

Bushing, Mary C. 1995. The library's product and excellence. *Library Trends* 43(winter): 384–400.

Carpenter, Beth. 1998. Your attention, please! Marketing today's libraries. *Computers in Libraries* 18(8): 62–66.

Cram, Jennifer. 1996. Benefiting the bottom line. *The Australian Library Journal* 45(Nov.): 300–307.

Crosby, Lawrence, and Sheree Johnson. 2001. Branding and your CRM strategy. *Marketing Management* 10(2): 6–7.

   About customer relationship management (CRM).

Curci-Gonzalez, Luci. 2000. All I really need to know about law library marketing I learned watching commercials during the Super Bowl. *AALL Spectrum* 4(6): 16.

Dimick, Barbara. 1995. Marketing youth services. *Library Trends* 43(3): 463–77.

Donald, Roslyn. 2001. Valuing library services. Available at <http://www.insitepro.com/donald2.htm>.

Gorchels, Linda M. 1995. Trends in marketing services. *Library Trends* 43 (winter): 494–509.

Greenawalt, Bethann. 2002. Can branding curb burnout? *Nursing Management* 32(9): 26–31.

Kassel, Amelia. 1999. How to write a marketing plan. *MLS: Marketing Library Services* 13(5). Available at <http://www.infotoday.com/mls/jun99/how-to.htm>.

Koontz, Christine M. 2002. Market segmentation: Grouping your clients. *MLS: Marketing Library Services* 16(4): 4–7.

McKnight, Michelynn. 1996. Field tips: Marketing the "full service" library. *National Network* 20(3): 10.

Persyn, Mary G. 2001. Focus groups: Another tool for library management. *AALL Spectrum* 6(4): 22–23.

Poynder, Richard. 1997. It's the brand, stupid! Add value and build on a brand name—lessons to learn in Web building. *Information Today* 14(5): 14–17.

Salzwedel, Beth A., and Ellen Wilson Green. 2000. Planning and marketing. In *The Medical Library Association Guide to Managing Health Care Libraries*, edited by Ruth Holst and Sharon A. Phillips. New York: Neal-Schuman.

Siess, Judith A. 1998. Marketing 102: Some immutable laws. *The One-Person Library: A Newsletter for Librarians and Management* 15(5): 6–7.

———. 1999. User surveys. *The One-Person Library: A Newsletter for Librarians and Management* 15(10): 6.

Stear, Edward B. 1997. The successful manager: What business are you in? (Or who pushed Humpty-Dumpty?) *Online* 21(6): 83–86.

———. 1998. Live long and prosper: Aligning IRC [Information Research Center] strategies with the business. *Online* 22(2): 26–27.

Tennant, Roy. 2000. Co-branding and libraries. *Library Journal* 125(20): 40–42.

White, Herbert S. 1984. *Managing the special library: Strategies for success within the larger organization.* White Plains, N.Y.: Knowledge Industry.

Williamson, Joan. 1996. Connecting the organizational mission and the library mission. *The One-Person Library: A Newsletter for Librarians and Management* 12(9): 3.

## WEBSITES

American Library Association—publicity products to go with the "@ Your Library" campaign: <http://cs.ala.org/@yourlibrary/>

CIO CRM portal—Customer Resource Management (CRM) information from *CIO* (Chief Information Officer) magazine: <http://www.cio.com/research/crm/>

Colorado Library Marketing Council: <http://www.clmc.org>

Evelyn Daniel's Marketing Bibliography: <http://www.ils.unc.edu/daniel/237/readings2002.html>

IFLA Management and Marketing Section: <http://www.ifla.org/VII/s34/somm.htm>

LEXIS-NEXIS—"Marketing tips for information professionals: A practical workbook": <http://www.lexisnexis.com/infopro/reference/default.shtml>

Measuring the Difference, by Cathy Burroughs: <http://nnlm.gov/evaluation/guide>

Sheila Webber's Library and Information Marketing Site (UK): <http://dis.shef.ac.uk/sheila/marketing/>

Social Science Information Gateway (UK), Marketing Section: <http://www.sosig.ac.uk/roads/subject-listing/World-cat/market.html>

University of Texas Advertising World: <http://advertising.utexas.edu/world/>

Wilson Internet's Web Marketing and E-commerce—short practical articles, lots of links to other articles and sites: <http://www.wilsonweb.com/>

# CHAPTER 3. PUBLICITY: THE TANGIBLES

## BOOK

Karp, Rashelle S. 2002. Powerful public relations: A how-to guide for libraries. Chicago: American Library Assn.

## ARTICLES

Baker, Lynda M., and Virginia Manbeck. 2002. Promoting the CHI collection and service. Chap 6. in *Consumer health information for public librarians*. Lanham, Md.: Scarecrow.

Balas, Janet L. 1999. The 'don'ts' of Web page design. *Computers in Libraries* 19(8): 46–48.

Buchanan, Leigh. 1999. The smartest little company in America: Highsmith Inc. uses a knowledge-management tool of extraordinary power to give employees all the information they need. Its name is Lisa Guedea Carreño. She's the librarian. *Inc.* (January): 43–54.

    The single best PR piece ever appearing for librarians.

Duncan, Moira. 1994. Totally unique!! How *not* to write a press release. *Managing Information* 1(9): 39–40.

Ekhaml, Leticia. 1997. Tell it to the public! *School Library Media Activities Monthly* 14(10): 28–29.

Fialkoff, Francine, and Evan St. Lifer. 2002. Putting libraries in the headlines. *Netconnect* (supplement to *Library Journal*) (summer): 2.

Glinert, Susan 1999. Top of the ranks. *Home Office Computing* 17(11): 105-6.

Guenther, Kim. 1999. Publicity through better Web site design. *Computers in Libraries* 19(8): 62–67.

Hordie, Julia. 2002. No business like self-promotion. *Information World Review* (181): 28.

Paul, Meg. 1999. How does your promotional material rate? *The One-Person Library: A Newsletter for Librarians and Management* 15(10): 5–6.

Raeder, Aggi. 1997. Promoting your Web site. *Searcher* 5(July/Aug.): 63–66.

Rowley, Jennifer. 1998. Promotion and marketing communications in the information marketplace. *Library Review* 47(8): 383–87.

Siess, Judith A. 1999a. Ideas for bulletin boards on a shoestring. *The One-Person Library: A Newsletter for Librarians and Management* 15(8): 6–7.

———. 1999b. Suggestions for library bulletin boards. *The One-Person Library: A Newsletter for Librarians and Management* 15(8): 8–9.

———. 1999c. Celebrating special days. *The One-Person Library: A Newsletter for Librarians and Management* 15(10): 4–5.

———. 1999d. Tips for a better library Web site. *The One-Person Library: A Newsletter for Librarians and Management* 16(7): 7–10.

Toch, M. Uri, and Tom Farmer. 2002. Promote libraries with electronic newsletters. *MLS: Marketing Library Services* 16(2/3): 5–6.

Wagner, Pat. 2001. Secrets of a successful presenter. *Info Career Trends* 2(5). Available at <http://www.lisjobs.com>.

Wreden, Nick. 2002. How to make your case in thirty seconds or less. *Harvard Management Communication Letter* 5(1): 10–11.

Zach, Lisl. 2002. A librarian's guide to speaking the business language. *Information Outlook* 6(6): 18–24.

## WEBSITES

American Library Association—posters, bookmarks, and so forth, and a press kits page: <http://www.ala.org/pio/presskits/>

Association of Research Libraries—twenty-one-page guide to media relations: <http://www.arl.org/mediamap.pdf>

Clip Art—$10 to $15 per graphic, from Chris Olson & Associates: <http://www.libraryclipart.com>

Factiva—information on marketing the information center (including finding time and money for marketing, marketing ideas and techniques, and a sample marketing plan): <http://www.factiva.com/infopro/resource3.asp?node=right1>

Gale Group—marketing support, downloadable leaflets: <http://www.gale.com/free_resources/marketing/support/index.htm>

Innovative Internet Applications in Libraries: <http://www.wiltonlibrary.org/innovate.html>

Joe Ryan's Information Resources for Information Professionals: <http://web.syr.edu/~jryan/infopro/public.html>

Stephanie Stokes Design, Library Media, and PR Site: <http://www.ssdesign.com/librarypr/>

3M: How to Market @ Your Library: Creating Your Five-Year Campaign—manual (in PDF format): <http://www.3m.com/market/security/library/whatsnew/webcast.jhtml>

Writing a marketing plan: <http://www.insitepro.com/donald3.htm>

# CHAPTER 4. PUBLIC RELATIONS: THE PERSONAL TOUCH

## BOOKS

Donahue, Karin V., Sandra S. Gold, Janice E. Henderson, Loretta Mak, Alice McKenzie, and Gitelle Seer. 1999. *Managing the law library 1999: Forging effective relationships in today's law office.* Intellectual Property Course Handbook Series, G-546. New York: Practising Law Institute.

Fleming, Neil. 2002. *Fifty-five strategies for better teaching.* Christchurch, New Zealand. Neil Fleming.
    A wonderful resource (order at <http://www.vark-learn.com>).

Wolfe, Lisa A. 1997. *Library public relations, promotions, and communications: A how-to-do-it manual for librarians.* New York: Neal-Schuman.

## ARTICLES

Block, Marylaine. 2000. Training our bosses. *Ex Libris: An E-Zine for Librarians and Other Information Junkies.* (Mar.). Available at <http://marylaine.com/exlibris/>.

Bumgarner, Elizabeth A. 2000. A virtual open house. *MLS: Marketing Library Services* 14(8). Available at <http://www.infotoday.com/mls/dec00/bumgarner.htm>.

Hammond, Patricia. 2000. Courting the medical staff. *MLA News* (322): 13.

Hurst, Jill Ann. 2001. A tourist in the library. *The One-Person Library: A Newsletter for Librarians and Management* 18(3): 14–15.

Mileham, Patricia, Joan Ruelle, and Susan Sykes Berry. 2002. Playing well with others: Increasing your library-campus partnerships. *Collection Management* 26(3): 77–87.

Nims, Julia. 1999. Marketing the library instruction services: Changes and trends. *Reference Services Review* 27(3): 249–53.

## WEB SITES

ALA promotional events page, links to information and supporting material for events such as Teen Read Week:
    <http://www.ala.org/events/promoevents/>

Library Instruction—some great resources and links for better teaching. Especially good is Michael Lorenzen's "Working with Adult Learners in the Library Classroom: A Personal Reflection" (2002): <http://www.libraryinstruction.com>

# CHAPTER 5. ADVOCACY: PUTTING IT ALL TOGETHER

## Advocacy and Professionalism

### BOOKS

Akey, Stephen. 2002. *Library.* Washington, D.C.: Orchises.

> Fascinating, irreverent look at librarianship in large public libraries. There are some good observations hidden in this train-of-thought book.

Boccialetti, Gene. 1995. *It takes two: Managing yourself when working with bosses and other authority figures.* San Francisco: Jossey-Bass.

Hall, Richard B. 1995. *Winning library referenda campaigns: A how-to-do-it manual.* New York: Neal-Schuman.

### ARTICLES

Bridgman, Tracy Gray. 2002. Taking advantage of Friends groups. *AALL Spectrum* 6(7): 20.

Corcoran, Mary. 2002. How to survive and thrive in the new economy: Follow the money. *Online* 26(3): 76–77.

Diprose, Kym. 1997. Pricing the invaluable: Putting a value on information in the corporate context. *The Australian Library Journal* (Nov.): 386–93.

Ebbinghouse, Carol. 2002. Would you hire you? Continuing education for the information professional. *Searcher* 10(7): 110–15.

Flood, Gary. 2002. Pinpointing the price of information. *Information World Review* (180): 9.

> Interview with Clare Hart, president of Factiva.

Harhai, Marilyn Kay. 2002. Maybe it's not too late to join the circus: Books for midlife career management. *Library Trends* 50(4): 640–50.

Henczel, Susan. 2001. Developing business savvy—applying our library competencies to the business environment. *The One-Person Library: A Newsletter for Librarians and Management* 18(7): 8–9.

Holt, Glen E. 1996. On becoming essential: An agenda for quality in twenty-first century public libraries. *Library Trends* 43(winter): 545–71.

Hotchkiss, Mary A. 1988. Managing multiple projects, or the art of juggling. *AALL Spectrum* 3(1): 12.

Houdek, Frank G., comp. 1997. A day in my law library life. *Law Library Journal* 89: 157–223.

How do you manage? Regular *Library Journal* column appearing in every other issue.

Jacobs, Leslie, and Mary Corcoran. 2002. Lessons from library closings. *Information Briefing* 5(9): 1–9.

Justis, Janet. 2001. Before you visit your legislator review some tips from the advocacy gurus. *Virginia Libraries* 47(3): 913.

Kearns, Kevin P. 1997. Managing upward: Working effectively with supervisors and others in the hierarchy. *Information Outlook* 1(10): 23–27.

Krattenmaker, Tom. 2002. A blueprint for constructing a personal and professional network. *Harvard Management Communication Letter* 5(4): 6–7.

Landry-Hyde, Denise. 2002. Lifelong learning. *Info Career Trends* 3(2).

Lettis, Lucy. 1999. Be proactive: Communicate your worth to management. *Information Outlook* 3(1): 25–29.

> Includes a long list of competencies she's developed for junior-level information specialists.

Marshall, Joanne Gard. 2000. Determining our worth, communicating our value. *Library Journal* (Nov. 15): 28–29.

McClary, Pat. 2001. Planning for success at the election polls. *MLS: Marketing Library Services* 15(8): 1–3.

McKnight, Michelynn. 2002. Sharing our worth. *National Network* 26(3): 1, 4.

Perley, Cathy M. 2002. Reflections on hospital library services in ambulatory settings. *Journal of Hospital Librarianship* 2(1): 19–27.

Riley, Bryan. 2000. Demonstrating value in a competitive environment. *InCite* 21(4): 14.

Spohr, Cindy. 2001. Speakeasy: The art of communicating value. *AALL Spectrum* 6(40): 36.

Toftoy, Charles N. 2002. The key to a librarian's success: Developing entrepreneurial traits. *Information Outlook* 6(6): 42–47.

van der Voort, Sara. 1998. Are you into analysis? Remember to emphasize the value you add! *Online* (Jan./Feb.): 58–60.

White, Herbert S. 1984. *Managing the special library: Strategies for success within the larger organization.* White Plains, N.Y.: Knowledge Industry.

> Especially the articles "Public Libraries and the Political Process" and "Toward Professionalism."

Zemon, Candy Bogar. 2002. Midlife career choices: How are they different from other career choices? *Library Trends* 50(4): 665–72.


## WEBSITES

ALA, Library Advocate's Handbook—advice about how to put forward the case for your library:
<http://www.ala.org/pio/advocacy/libraryadvocateshandbook.pdf>

Freedman Better Salaries and Pay Equity Task Force Website:
<http://www.mjfreedman.org/tftext.html>

On the Image of Librarians and Libraries, by Jennifer Cram:
<http://www.alia.org.au/~jcram/image_librarians.html>


## *Career Planning*

### BOOKS

Boldt, L. D. 1999. *Zen and the art of making a living: A practical guide to creative career design.* Rev. ed. New York: Penguin/Arkana.

Bolles, R. N. 2000. *What color is your parachute? A practical manual for jobhunters and career changers.* 30th anniversary ed. Berkeley: Ten Speed Pr.

> Considered a classic for job hunters.

Helfand, D. P. 1999. *Career change: Everything you need to know to meet new challenges and take control of your career.* 2d ed. Lincolnwood, Ill.: VGM Career Horizons.

Nesbeitt, Sarah L., and Rachel Singer Gordon. 2002. *The information professional's guide to career development online.* Medford, N.J.: Information Today.

Pantry, Sheila, and Peter Griffiths. 1999. *Your successful LIS career: Planning your career, CVs, interviews and self-promotion.* London: Library Assn.

> Examples are mostly from the United Kingdom, but the ideas are applicable everywhere.

Podesta, Connie, and Jean Gatz. 1997. *How to be the person successful companies fight to keep: The insider's guide to being #1 in the workplace.* New York: Simon & Schuster.

Rausch, Erwin, and John Washbush. 1998. *High quality leadership: Practical guidelines to becoming a more effective manager.* Milwaukee, Wis.: American Society for Quality/Quality Pr.

Roy, Loriene, and Antony Cherian. 2002. *Getting libraries the credit they deserve: A Festschrift in honor of Marvin H. Scilken*. Lanham, Md.: Scarecrow.

Salmon, W. A., and R. Salmon. 2000. *The mid-career tune-up: Ten new habits for keeping your edge in today's fast-paced workplace*. New York: American Management Assn.

## ARTICLES

Harhai, Marilyn Kay. 2002. Maybe it's not too late to join the circus: Books for midlife career management. *Library Trends* 50(4): 640–50.

Whisner, Mary. 1999. Choosing law librarianship: Thoughts for people contemplating a career move. Available at <http://www.llrx.com/features/librarian.htm>.

   LLRX is the Law Library Resource Xchange.

## WEBSITES

Ann's Place: Library Job Hunting:
   <http://www.geocities.com/aer_ mcr/libjob/>

BUBL News—library and information science jobs:
   <http://www.bubl.ac.uk/news/jobs>

Chronicle of Higher Education—Career Network:
   <http://chronicle.com/jobs>

Library Job Postings on the Internet: <http://www.libraryjobpostings.org>

The Networked Librarian Employment Resources for Librarians:
   <http://pw2.netcom.com/~feridun/nlintro.htm>

# INDEX

**Judith A. Siess** is a recognized expert in one-person librarianship and interpersonal networking. She has drawn from her more than twenty years' experience and written *The SOLO Librarian's Sourcebook* (Information Today, 1997); *The OPL Sourcebook* (Information Today, 2001); and *Time Management, Planning and Prioritization for Librarians* (Scarecrow, 2002). Siess has been the editor and publisher of *The One-Person Library: A Newsletter for Librarians and Management* since 1998 and is the author of articles for publications such as *American Libraries* and *Searcher.* An active member of SLA, she was the inaugural chair of its SOLO Librarian's division, which is now the fourth largest division of the association with more than 1,000 members. Siess conducts workshops for continuing professional education in the United States and abroad.